AF215309

Contents

Welcome to your wild and wonderful brain!

Having ADHD can be exciting, frustrating, joyful, confusing and so many other things, sometimes all in the same day! I know, because I have it myself. Some people talk about ADHD as if it's either a terrible curse or an incredible superpower, but neither of those things feel right to me.

When I put something down and can't find it again for a week, ADHD doesn't feel like a superpower. It feels like a total pain. And when my brain fizzles and sparks with curiosity and creative ideas, it certainly doesn't feel like a curse! It's magical and exciting and really great fun.

What my brain feels, to me, is WILD. A stubborn, mysterious, unpredictable force of nature that won't follow the rules of how the world often seems to think a

Alice Harman

Illustrated by
Buse Kaçar

YOUR WILD AND WONDERFUL BRAIN

MAKE YOUR UNIQUE ADHD BRAIN WORK FOR YOU!

BLOOMSBURY
CHILDREN'S BOOKS
LONDON OXFORD NEW YORK NEW DELHI SYDNEY

For my husband, David – A.H.

To my daughter, my husband
and my sisters – B.K.

BLOOMSBURY CHILDREN'S BOOKS
Bloomsbury Publishing Plc
50 Bedford Square, London WC1B 3DP, UK
Bloomsbury Publishing Ireland Limited
29 Earlsfort Terrace, Dublin 2, D02 AY28, Ireland

BLOOMSBURY, BLOOMSBURY CHILDREN'S BOOKS and the Diana logo
are trademarks of Bloomsbury Publishing Plc

First published in Great Britain in 2026 by Bloomsbury Publishing Plc

Text copyright © Alice Harman, 2026
Illustrations copyright © Buse Kaçar, 2026
Expert consultant: Dr Valeria Parlatini
Sensitivity readers: Lex Academic

Alice Harman and Buse Kaçar have asserted their rights under the Copyright,
Designs and Patents Act, 1988, to be identified as Author and Illustrator of this work

A catalogue record for this book is available from the British Library

ISBN: PB: 978-1-5266-9441-6
eBook: 978-1-5266-9442-3; Audio: 978-1-5266-9448-5
2 4 6 8 10 9 7 5 3 1
Printed and bound in Great Britain by Clays Ltd, Elcograf S.p.A

To find out more about our authors and books,
visit www.bloomsbury.com and sign up for our newsletters

For product safety related questions, contact productsafety@bloomsbury.com

brain 'should' work. I can't bully or beg it into being tamed, can't force it to do things the way that most brains seem to. And, actually, I don't want to!

There is nothing WRONG with my brain. There is nothing WRONG with your brain. It's not worse, or better, than anyone else's. It just has its own unique strengths and struggles, which we can learn to work with rather than fighting against. This book is designed to be a guide to help you do just that – in a fun, totally non-judgemental, ADHD-friendly way.

Of course, every person's brain is different, and that's true among people with ADHD, too. So not everything in this book will feel relevant to you, and not every idea or activity will work for you. You know your own wild and wonderful brain best, so feel totally free to take what feels helpful and skip the rest!

Why I wrote this book

I'm not a doctor or an ADHD expert leading cutting-edge research (or anything remotely like that)! But as someone with ADHD, who was only **diagnosed** as an adult, I've spent my life figuring out how to work with my brain — and I've learned a lot from my mistakes along the way. It's not been easy, but my wild brain has managed to write more than 50 books (despite STILL protesting every time I sit down at my computer ...), so I guess I must be doing something right! Although there are still ups and downs, and there probably always will be, me and my ADHD brain are getting along much better than we used to.

I wanted to write this book to give people like you the book that I wish I had myself at that age. To give you a realistic view of living with ADHD, acknowledging both the challenges and brilliant bits, and to use the skills I've learned as a writer to create a (hopefully) helpful and insightful book. There's SO much more information out there about ADHD than when I was a kid — some of it great, and some a bit ... less great. The content of this book is research-based, along with some personal reflections, ideas and practical strategies that I've found helpful. It has also been reviewed by specialist ADHD consultant, Dr Valeria Parlatini.

I really hope that you enjoy reading this book and find some ideas that make things a bit easier for you and your brain. More than anything, though, I hope that you understand how brilliant you are – just as you are! Because learning to genuinely accept and support yourself – rather than trying to force or shame yourself into following society's invented 'musts' and 'shoulds' when they just don't work for you – is life-changing. It's what you and your wild and wonderful brain deserve!

Read on for some key terms and phrases that will come up in the book, including a quick look at the three recognised types of ADHD.

Not everyone reading this book will have an ADHD **diagnosis**, but of course you're absolutely welcome here, too! Maybe you're exploring and learning more about ADHD because you think you may have it yourself? Or because you want to better understand and support someone who does? Whatever the reason, it's lovely to have you! Just please make sure that you, or the person you have in mind, is getting proper care from medical professionals – when it comes to understanding your brain and how it works, you should never have to manage alone.

What is ADHD?

A person with ADHD may focus on tasks differently compared to others their age, may switch attention more quickly and may often forget or misplace things. In medical definitions, these are often known as 'attention problems'. They could also find it hard to control their impulses (sudden strong desires to do something) and always be on the go. In medical definitions, these are often called '**impulsivity** and **hyperactivity** problems'.

Medical definitions of ADHD tend to focus on the aspects that can be more difficult for people to manage, but – as we'll see in this book – ADHD can also be associated with very positive things, from super-creative thinking to tons of enthusiastic energy! Lots of famous and highly respected people have ADHD, from musicians and Olympic athletes to scientists and top business owners. Many have talked about how they think their ADHD is part of what's made them so successful!

The three types of ADHD

The three officially recognised types (or presentations) of ADHD are:

- **predominantly inattentive ADHD**
- **predominantly hyperactive-impulsive ADHD**
- **combined ADHD**

People with predominantly **inattentive ADHD** can often find it harder than non-ADHD people to:

- **hold their attention on tasks and activities**
- **give close attention to details and notice little mistakes**
- **listen when spoken to directly**
- **follow through on instructions and finish tasks**
- **get and stay organised**
- **resist distractions**
- **remember what they're doing and what people have said**
- **not lose things**

People with predominantly **hyperactive-impulsive ADHD** can often find it harder than non-ADHD people to:

- **sit still, and keep their hands and feet still**
- **stay seated when asked or expected to**
- **relax and be quiet**
- **manage their racing thoughts**
- **wait until a question is completed (or until someone has finished talking) before speaking**
- **wait to take turns, to be asked to speak or to join in**

People with **combined type ADHD** (like me!) have both inattentive and hyperactive-impulsive **traits**. This means they can find it harder to do a mix of the things mentioned above than people without ADHD.

Although everyone may find some of these things tricky, people with ADHD can find that they affect how we manage at school and in our social life. ADHD usually first shows up in childhood, and some of us show fewer traits as we grow older. (Remember, medical descriptions of ADHD tend to focus on things we can find tricky, rather than our strengths, so they can sound very one-sided!)

Some people with ADHD choose to take medication to help them with their **symptoms**. This is a completely personal choice, based on each **ADHDer's** own experience and medical history — neither way is right or wrong! It's something that you need to discuss with a doctor or other medical expert. I'm not a doctor, so I don't really talk about medication at all in this book.

How to use this book

Each chapter of this book focuses on a different ADHD **trait**, represented by an animal, and starts by looking at the related strengths and struggles that people with that trait might experience. Then, we move on to some ideas for working with our brain to help us through the struggles and boost — or just appreciate — the strengths!

Throughout the book, you'll find 'did you know?' boxes filled with facts alongside fun 'side quest' mini activities. These are to keep things ADHD-friendly, as our brains tend to love a mix of new, different things! There's also a 'brain break' section at the end of every chapter. Here you'll find games, riddles, quizzes, creative activities, fascinating animal facts, as well as ideas for answering challenging (or even slightly irritating) questions about your ADHD. You'll also find plenty of bite-sized 'brain science' facts throughout the book to learn more about the science behind ADHD and discover why our brains might work in the wild ways they do.

It might be helpful to grab a new notebook (or open a new digital note or document if you prefer that) to scribble down any thoughts or ideas you have as you read. If you want to try out any practical strategies, you can also add them to your notebook to help you remember what to do and to note how well they work for you. The activities are all just for fun, so you can do them in your notebook or just on a scrap piece of paper. Just don't write in the book if it's not yours or you're not allowed!

If you're not sure what a word means, you can always check the key terms on the next page. You can also flick to the glossary (page 258), which includes more words – all of these words are in bold throughout the book.

Right, are you ready to start exploring your wild and wonderful ADHD brain? Turn the page and let's go!

Key terms

- **ADHDer**: an informal/non-medical way of describing someone who has ADHD, which I use throughout this book

- **AuDHD**: an informal term for someone who is autistic and also has ADHD

- **burnout**: feeling extremely tired, empty and unable to do anything more

- **diagnosis**: when a doctor, or other health professional, officially identifies that someone has a particular condition (such as ADHD)

- **genetics**: the science of how different traits – from eye colour to some medical conditions – can be passed down from parent to child through our genes, which are tiny parts of our body's cells

- **hyperactivity**: being extremely active and energetic

- **hyperfocus**: a state of intense concentration that can last for hours and hours on end

- **impulsivity**: acting quickly, without thinking things through

- **masking**: hiding parts of yourself, including your ADHD traits, to fit in with others and avoid negative reactions

- **mental health**: how someone is feeling in their mind and emotions

- **neurodivergent**: when someone thinks, learns or behaves differently to what society sees as 'typical'. People with ADHD may consider themselves neurodivergent. Neurodiversity is the idea that everyone's brain is different, and that we all experience and react to the world in different, equally valuable ways. Everyone is neurodiverse (including neurotypical people), but some people use this word in the same way as 'neurodivergent'

- **neurotypical**: when someone thinks, learns and/or behaves in ways that society sees as 'typical'

- **self-esteem**: how we feel about ourselves, and how valuable we think we are

- **stimming**: making repeating movements or sounds, with your body or objects, often without realising. Common stims (short for 'self-stimulatory behaviours') include playing with a pen, rocking, twirling your hair, tapping your foot or humming

- **symptom**: a physical or mental effect or trait that someone experiences because of a medical condition

- **unmasking**: when you stop hiding parts of yourself, including your ADHD traits, to fit in with others

- **well-being**: feeling healthy, comfortable and generally happy or content

Chapter one
Magpie

Magpie
Being distracted by shiny new things

Struggle

Ooh, shiny! For centuries, people have told tales of magpies thieving everything from coins, keys and glittering jewellery to bottle caps, ring pulls and gleaming pebbles. Supposedly, the birds simply can't resist anything with a bit of sparkle, and will drop everything to stash these shiny treasures in their nests.

ADHDers may recognise their own shiny-seeking impulses here! How many times have you been distracted by shiny new ideas, projects or interests, instead of working on something that you've already started? (If you're anything like me, very often!)

It can feel like an irresistible rush of enthusiasm and energy is pushing us to explore these sparkly new paths.

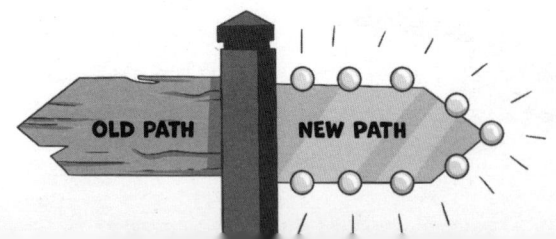

By comparison, continuing with our original plan feels like an impossibly dull, difficult trudge — even if the end is in sight, and the goal once felt just as excitingly shiny.

Although people without ADHD can also experience this attraction towards the new and intriguing, research suggests that ADHDers may feel it more strongly. We tend to be more **impulsive**, too: we may do things as soon as they occur to us, rather than taking time to think them through. This may make it harder for us to resist the lure of the shiny, new thing and just carry on with the task in hand.

Impulsiveness is explored in the Salmon chapter on page 87.

All this can mean that we might not finish or make much progress with things, particularly long-term projects, which can feel disheartening. We may end up with so many half-finished projects or semi-abandoned interests that it feels **overwhelming** and stressful.

When we lose interest in something that we were once so passionate about, we may feel like our time, effort and possibly money has been wasted, and be annoyed at ourselves. We may even be embarrassed if we've talked excitedly to other people about our 'new thing' and, when they ask about it, we have to admit that we've dropped it.

Strength

Magpies are believed to be some of the most intelligent animals in the world. They can make and use tools, imitate human speech, work in teams and even recognise themselves in mirrors. It seems that magpies' natural **inquisitiveness**, along with their **adaptability** and interest in problem-solving, is key to many of their impressive skills.

Curiosity, enthusiasm and fascination with the world around us are all absolutely priceless strengths. Yes, we might be pulled off-course by shiny new interests, but I can't imagine living life without that sparkle! That overwhelming excitement and unexpected delight can make us feel so connected to the world and all its incredible potential.

The first 'Ooh, shiny!' intensity might not last forever, but that doesn't mean it's not real or valuable.

ADHDers' tendency towards 'novelty seeking' (seeking new things) could even help to keep our minds open to new possibilities and new ways of thinking and doing things. It can also be more **motivating** and inspiring for others than you might realise.

A 'neophiliac' is someone who finds new things **fulfilling** and exciting. How much of a neophiliac are you?

1. Which weekend plan sounds best to you?

A) Being taken to a new surprise activity that you've never done before
B) Spending the day enjoying your hobbies with friends, then stopping by your favourite restaurant

2. Would you rather ...

A) Watch as many new movies as you want, but not be able to rewatch your favourite five movies?
B) Rewatch your favourite five movies as much as you want, but not be able to watch any new movies?

3. Which of these sounds like your idea of a great holiday?

A) Going to a country you've never visited, on the other side of the world
B) Revisiting somewhere you've been before and where you have lots of happy memories

The more A) answers you gave, the more neophiliac you may be! If you gave all or mostly B) answers, you may be 'neophobic': someone who finds new things uncomfortable and prefers the familiar.

Remember, everyone is unique and there is no right or wrong way to be – and this quiz isn't scientific, it's just for fun!

Working with your brain

There is absolutely nothing wrong with being curious and excited about shiny new ideas, projects and interests! This joyful exploring can lead us to great things, and provide a lot of fun along the way.

However, we don't want to **overwhelm** ourselves, give up too quickly on things that bring us happiness, or miss out on the satisfaction of seeing our knowledge, skills and achievements grow over time.

Wait a second

When something new and shiny catches your attention and you want to drop whatever you're doing to pursue it, take a few seconds to think. Is it because you genuinely aren't enjoying your current project and you think your new idea is better? Or do you still like and believe in what you're currently doing, but find you've got to a point where it feels hard to keep going? Try to be honest with yourself!

If it's just that your current task feels hard at the moment, you might regret dropping it — especially if it's something that's been important to you. Even the things we like and do best can feel really difficult sometimes. Maybe, temporarily, they don't feel like that much fun. (I love writing, but I definitely have days when I feel like giving up!)

If you keep going, you might reach a new stage that's even more fun and satisfying.

Self-esteem support

Research has repeatedly shown that people with ADHD are more likely to have low **self-esteem**. We may often think more negatively about ourselves, and what we can and can't achieve. Ask yourself this: do you actually want to drop an activity because you don't believe you can do it? If the answer is 'yes', then well done on being honest with yourself! This is a great opportunity to show yourself that you can do hard things.

Make sure you ask for some support, though. A trusted adult can help you break down the task into steps that feel more manageable, and make a confidence-boosting 'I can do this' list.

You can find extra resources to help you on pages 241–257.

Reality check

Let's say you're working on a group project. **ADHDers** tend to be particularly good at coming up with lots of new, original ideas for the same problem — so it's very possible (and positive!) that while you're working on a task, you may suddenly have a better, shinier idea of how to do it completely differently. However, people with ADHD often experience time agnosia — a difference in how we sense, estimate and manage time — so we have to make sure we're not overloading ourselves (or others).

Ask someone to help you list out all the extra work that this change in direction would mean. Then work out together how much longer this would realistically take, making sure to overestimate the time needed.
(I typically double or triple my first guess!)

Do you have enough time before the project is due? Is everyone OK with any extra work? Sometimes, after thinking it all through, you'll find that the new, shiny way will actually save time and be less work — but this won't always be the case!

Give it a minute

The rush of excitement and focus that you get when you have a 'shiny new interest' can be really fun. It might even help you make a lot of progress quickly, which feels good and may mean you enjoy it even more. Great!

However, try just giving that wave of excitement a chance to wash over you. Before you make any big commitments, see if what's left on the other side of the **dopamine** rush is genuine interest. Is there a way to do some free taster sessions of a hobby, for instance? Could you talk to someone with experience in something that you think you might like to do?

The 'shiny' cycle

You're allowed to approach things differently from the way other people do! For instance, you may like to cycle through a few different hobbies or interests rather than always keeping up the same one. After a bit of time away, familiar things might start looking 'shiny' again.

BASKETBALL TASTER SESSION! 5 P.M.

As long as it works with the time you have, your existing commitments and the money your family has to spend on any kit or lessons, why not keep more than one hobby on the go? Surely that's better than giving up something that you enjoy because you slogged away at it until you hated it! Just be aware that you may make slower progress compared to others who go consistently, and that there's nothing wrong with that.

Prompting your memory can help you keep this up. For ADHD brains, the way our memory works can mean that the saying 'out of sight, out of mind' is very real! Research suggests that we respond well to visual reminders, like a basketball left out in view on a low shelf rather than put away in a cupboard.

If an interest has become less 'shiny' and appealing, this easy access means that you could more easily and **spontaneously** have a quick go. This could also act as a low-pressure way of getting back into things that have felt hard, and that you may have started avoiding because you're scared of 'failing' at them.

Brain break

Facts, games and ADHD-friendly activities to give your brain a rest

Most magpies belong to a family of birds called 'corvids', which also includes crows, jays and other species. Corvids are wildly intelligent — more so than scientists thought was possible without having a brain structure like ours. Although their brains are smaller and differently shaped to human brains, they are densely packed with **neurons**. This allows them to achieve the same complex feats of intelligence as **primates.**

Australian magpies are not part of the corvid family, but they're very intelligent, too. They've been seen working in teams to solve problems — including pecking off tracking devices that researchers have put on them!

Side quest

How many different shiny things can you think of in one minute? Set a timer and see how many you can scribble down before it goes off!

Did you know?

In the UK, it is a traditional belief that seeing a single magpie brings bad luck. In fact, a popular rhyme about magpies starts, 'One for sorrow, two for joy'. To cancel out this bad luck, superstitious people might say, 'How's your wife, Mr Magpie?'

There are different versions of this saying, and some ask after the magpie's children, too!

You're not hyper, so how can you have ADHD?

Despite the 'H' in ADHD standing for 'hyperactive', not all ADHDers are especially active and energetic. People with **inattentive ADHD** (see page 10), which is also the most common type in women and girls, don't tend to be hyperactive at all.

Physical hyperactivity can also be quite subtle, like someone tapping their foot or twirling their hair, rather than running and jumping around. Internal hyperactivity, such as racing thoughts and feelings of restlessness, often looks like daydreaming or being quiet to others. Many ADHDers don't get the support they need because their **traits** don't fit with people's expectations of what hyperactivity looks like.

Brain science

Although there isn't a single 'ADHD gene', family and twin studies suggest that ADHD often tends to run in families. One study found that if you have a sibling with ADHD, you are nine times more likely to have ADHD as well.

Magpies don't really like collecting shiny objects! A 2014 study showed that wild magpies are naturally neophobic, so unfamiliar objects — shiny or not — startle them rather than draw their interest. However, magpies do have their own 'shiny thing' that'll distract and consume their attention ... food! They eat all sorts of things and will boldly investigate food sources — they'll even peck open bin bags and steal from picnic tables.

So, a diamond necklace won't do much for them, but a glistening, sugar-glazed doughnut is the kind of shiny object that'll catch a magpie's eye!

Chapter two
Squirrel

Squirrel

Forgetting things quickly

Struggle

Squirrels are the quick, clever acrobats of the animal world, scurrying up tall tree trunks and leaping between high branches in search of the best nuts. However, scientists have found that – after all that hard work – squirrels may leave up to three quarters of their nut stash in the ground! Experts think some nuts might be abandoned deliberately, but squirrels almost certainly just forget where others are buried!

Many people with ADHD can likely relate to this, as we often experience memory differences. In fact, forgetfulness and losing or misplacing things are core **traits** that experts look for when **diagnosing** ADHD.

There are many types of memory. For instance, prospective memory is used to remember future tasks you need to do (like going to appointments), whereas recalling recent facts or events after a short period of time has passed is part of delayed memory. Lots of people with ADHD experience differences with various memory types, and our biggest and most common difference appears to be with **working memory**.

Working memory is how we hold recent information in our minds, often for only a short time, and then use it to complete a particular task. For example, you use your working memory when a teacher tells you which materials you need to go and collect for an art project.

Executive functions (see page 197), which include **working memory,** are often different in people with ADHD. Studies have shown that some areas in the prefrontal cortex (the part of the brain responsible for these functions) are less active in people with ADHD. This may explain why many of us experience differences with working memory.

ADHDers can find it difficult to hold information in our minds, even for very short amounts of time. This can sometimes make it challenging for us to follow verbal information – anything from a teacher's instructions to someone giving us directions or telling us a phone number. It may also mean that we forget where we've put something, even if we've just had it.

What number comes next in the sequence below?

06 68 88

Answer: 87 – turning the numbers upside
down gives 87, 88, 89, 90.

Strength

Can you guess a very positive outcome of squirrels forgetting where they've left their nuts and leaving them buried underground? Trees! Lots of trees!

Although many people with ADHD (including me!) may find memory differences discouraging, there can be some unexpected positive side effects. Not being able to rely on our memories pushes us to be creative problem-solvers, and develop our own systems and strategies for keeping track of everything. With this experience and insight, we can create similar systems to be applied elsewhere, helping others too.

People who find it easy to remember things can be tempted to 'wing it', trusting that they'll remember everything from key information to complex instructions. Much easier in the short-term, but risky! No one's memory is perfect, and there's no backup if something slips your mind and you're not prepared.

Professionals such as doctors, nurses, pilots and safety inspectors, who know that people's lives depend on them doing their jobs accurately, use carefully created systems with various checklists. They know that it can be dangerous to rely on memory alone, even for simple tasks that they do all the time. Mistakes happen, especially when you're working quickly and under pressure, so clear and thorough systems can literally save lives.

Even in situations that aren't 'life or death', it can help to develop and use systems rather than 'keeping it all in your head' – as people who find it easier to remember things may be tempted to do. Systems can make things more efficient, more reliable, less stressful and easier to work on as a team.

For example, many organisations use standard step-by-step instructions that explain how to do specific tasks. You don't have to remember all the details of how to do something, and try to explain them all to anyone else who needs to do it – you just write them down and update them as needed. Online workspaces for school projects, chore charts and other shared documents are common tools that make it easier to share information and keep clear records.

Creating and using these kinds of systems may seem like an unnecessary faff to someone used to relying on their good memory. They may need time to get used to them. However, to **ADHDers** – who've had to develop our own systems just to cope with daily life – they might be a helpful support (and mean we don't have to exhaust ourselves trying to remember everything). We might even have tips for improving them further!

Working with your brain

As many people with ADHD will know, not being able to rely on your memory can sometimes be a massive pain. It seems like actual magic to me when someone can ask for directions and then remember each step along the way, or hear about an event happening next week and just remember on the day when and where it's happening. I'd settle for not somehow losing a pencil that I had in my hand literally five seconds ago!

A lot of us keep pushing ourselves to 'just remember' – and then we feel disappointed when we forget things. But the thing is, shame and self-blame are not going to improve our memory. However, acknowledging the reality of our memory differences, and working with them, can make life so much easier! Here are some tactics you might find helpful:

Keep it simple

Trying to find things is stressful, annoying and takes up a lot of time. What can really help is reducing what you're asking of your memory by simplifying things in your daily life as much as possible. Many **ADHDers** find it helpful to be as **minimalist** as possible. Having less stuff around you can reduce messiness and feelings of being **overwhelmed**. It means there are fewer things to keep track of, too!

There's more about staying tidy in the Raccoon chapter on page 217.

Another way to keep things simple is to have a specific 'home' for important things, which go straight back there as soon as you've used them. For example, you could keep your water bottle in the side pocket of your bag, and put it back the moment you're finished with it. It may eventually become a habit, so you do it without thinking. What could you try this with?

I mostly wear only one coat (or jacket, in the summer) and use one bag, so I can leave things like headphones in my coat pocket and a pair of glasses in my bag. Then I don't have to remember to move them between other coats and bags. Simple!

Appreciate your efforts

There are things that we can do to support our memory, and even ways to improve it slightly. Regular exercise may help a bit, particularly team sports such as basketball where you have to keep track of what others are doing. Specific puzzle-based exercises for **working memory** can also help — try searching online for 'brain training' activities.

However, the reality is that memory issues associated with ADHD are the result of a genuine brain difference, and they probably won't ever go away entirely. It's not our fault, we're not just being careless, and it's not fair for people to assume that — especially if they know that we have ADHD.

The amount of effort that many of us put in to support our memory is so much more than is needed for just remembering something, as many people can. It isn't a sign that you don't care if you don't remember a friend's birthday — but it shows you REALLY care if you go to the effort of making and using a special system just so you won't forget. This should be appreciated — by yourself as much as anyone else!

GOOD JOB!

Brain break
Facts, games and ADHD-friendly activities to give your brain a rest

The Indian Giant Squirrel is the world's biggest known squirrel. At up to one metre long (including its tail), it's the length of an average goat — but much more colourful!

The squirrel's fabulous fur is a patchwork of red-brown, creamy yellow and shining purple-black. Scientists think this may actually help it camouflage itself against its multi-coloured forest home.

 Side quest

Have you ever tried a nature bingo walk? Go outdoors and look for the things below, then tick them off when you spot them. Don't touch them without an adult's permission, though — and don't touch wild animals at all!

something brown

something smooth

something tiny

a colourful leaf

something patterned

a bird   **an insect**

an interesting stone

something circle-shaped

Want a challenge? See if you or a friend can finish the list first! You could even make up your own things to look out for. The possibilities are endless!

Won't you just grow out of your ADHD symptoms?

It's possible, but most likely not! This misunderstanding of ADHD is still very common. That's probably because for a long time, ADHD was believed to affect only children, not adults. Scientists have now found that, while some children with ADHD stop showing symptoms as adults, up to 70 per cent will continue to experience them.

Even if you are one of the people who 'grows out of' your ADHD symptoms, or finds they are easier to manage as an adult, the important thing is that they are affecting you now. You need support and understanding, not people downplaying or dismissing your experience.

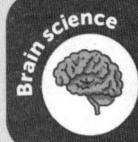

In a recent study, adults with ADHD were asked what they liked most about having ADHD. Some of the top answers were:

- being creative
- being curious
- trying new things
- being spontaneous
- finding solutions to problems
- being open-minded
- being empathetic
- having different perspectives on things

What do you like most about having ADHD?

Side quest

Turn a simple triangle into something new. Copy the shape as many times as you like, and let your imagination go wild! How many different things can you draw?

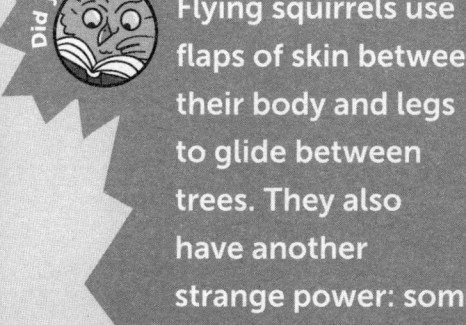

Did you know?

Flying squirrels use flaps of skin between their body and legs to glide between trees. They also have another strange power: some species glow bright pink under **ultraviolet (UV)** light!

Chapter three
Bee

Bee

Being very active and energetic

Strength

Not many animals are busier than bees! **Foraging** bees can visit up to 2,000 flowers a day to collect nectar and pollen. They may travel up to six kilometres away from their hives to find food, flapping their wings more than 200 times a second. We owe a lot to bees for their hard work, from the delicious honey they make to the many different plants that they pollinate.

ADHDers can be some of the busiest humans around, even if bees outdo us in the animal kingdom! Many of us find it really hard to stop (or even slow down) our super-charged brains and bodies. This tendency to be extremely active and energetic is known as **hyperactivity**.

We may love and excel at physical activities that stop our hyperactive bodies feeling twitchy and under-exercised. We also often have hyperactive brains that buzz with different thoughts about things we notice around us. This can inspire creativity and problem-solving efforts to change the world for the better.

Our energy and enthusiasm for life can be impressive: we can sometimes do so many things in a day that even just hearing about them would tire out some people!

Keeping our hyperactive brains or bodies happy can lead many ADHDers into exciting and **fulfilling** activities, and help us get the most out of each day. Our super-busy brains can totally immerse themselves in all sorts of different things – and have fun doing it!

Both our attraction to new experiences and **impulsive** tendencies can mean that we often jump straight into things! This can end up broadening our minds and enriching our lives with all sorts of interesting ideas and experiences.

You can read more about ADHDers' attraction to new things in the Magpie chapter on page 17 and impulsivity in the Salmon chapter on page 87.

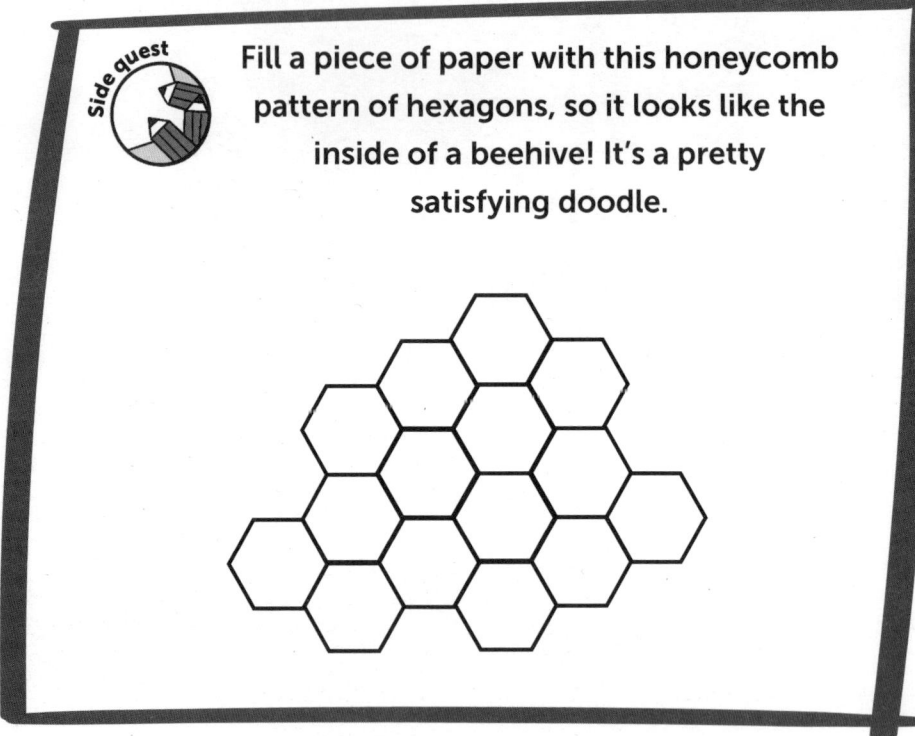

Side quest

Fill a piece of paper with this honeycomb pattern of hexagons, so it looks like the inside of a beehive! It's a pretty satisfying doodle.

Struggle

Have you ever seen a bee lying still or crawling slowly on the ground? This often happens because it has been so busy flying around for so long, without enough rest or nourishment, that it has completely exhausted itself.

This might sound familiar to some **ADHDers**! **Hyperactivity** can be hard on our busy bodies and brains. We sometimes don't notice when we need to slow down or rest, or we feel a strong urge to press on anyway.

This can eventually send us into a huge energy crash. We may find that, over time, continually wearing ourselves out can lead to a state of serious exhaustion, which some people call ADHD **burnout**.

ADHD **burnout** isn't a recognised medical term, but a lot of us find it useful to describe the experience of becoming so **overwhelmed** and exhausted over time that we 'burn out' and stop being able to function in basic ways. This can happen because we're trying to handle the day-to-day effort of supporting our ADHD **traits** while meeting the demands of a world designed for **neurotypical** people, on top of everything else we're trying to do.

The high energy of **hyperactivity** may sometimes feel helpful and fun. But at other times, you might want your brain or body to calm down — and they just won't. This can be frustrating, especially in situations where you're expected to be still (as you often are during the school day) or when you're trying to rest or sleep.

I know from personal experience that it can be physically uncomfortable and even painful when I need to get up and move around but feel a pressure to stay still — like when I'm watching a movie at the cinema or stuck as a passenger on a long car journey. (I get shooting pains in my legs and an all-over restlessness that feels like my skin's crawling or burning!) These strong feelings can be distracting, as can the endless loops of inner thoughts that can come with mental hyperactivity. They make it hard for me to stay connected to the world beyond my own mind and body.

Even when we are physically exhausted and want to rest, or we experience only mental hyperactivity, a racing mind in a still body isn't exactly relaxing. Many adults and children with ADHD experience disrupted sleep, and may struggle to both fall asleep and get out of bed in the morning. Lack of sleep affects our ability to focus and manage our emotions, and can have other long-term effects such as physical illness and changes in mood and behaviour. It's important to try to calm our minds before bedtime, as difficult as this may be, as it can really help our sleep. Some people like to take a bath, read, or listen to music or audiobooks. What helps you feel calm?

Working with your brain

A busy bee needs to rest and refuel sometimes, or it won't be able to carry on. Similarly, we **ADHDers** need to take care of ourselves. We need to find ways to rest that feel nourishing and that work for us. Many of us find common rest activities – watching TV, listening to music or simply lying down – not stimulating enough for our busy bodies and minds. Rather than feeling relaxed, we may feel bored and restless. We may even feel annoyed at ourselves for not being able to rest in the same way as others!

The resting 'sweet spot'

What can work better for some people with ADHD (including me!) is to practise finding a 'sweet spot' with just the right amount of stimulation. For example:

→ You could find an activity that feels engaging enough to hold your attention, but not so stressful that it doesn't feel like rest. For instance, I find action-filled video games too full-on, but more casual, relaxed ones tend to be just the right level for my brain.

→ You could alternate between higher- and lower-energy activities. For example, you could challenge yourself to follow a tricky dance routine video, and then flop on the sofa and read for a bit. When you get twitchy, you can switch back to the high-energy activity.

→ You could combine two or more traditional rest activities. For instance, you could do a craft (like sewing or model making) while watching TV, read with background music on, listen to an audiobook or podcast as you go for a gentle walk, or draw while talking with friends.

→ You could try something that might not be restful for someone else. For example, I sometimes find it really restful to paint a room, do a tough quiz (in person or on TV) or research a subject that has nothing to do with my life. Others might find things like writing music or baking muffins restful – but to me, that sounds like really hard work. Your rest activities don't have to make sense to anyone but you!

→ Keep experimenting! Remember that your 'sweet spot' will not only be unique to you, but might also change depending on things like mood, stress, energy levels and current interests.

Different types of rest

A popular modern theory, developed by Dr Saundra Dalton-Smith, is that humans actually need seven different types of rest. This idea may be helpful for some **ADHDers**, as it gives us 'permission' to rest in more active ways when stillness isn't working for us.

It can be tricky to know what kind of rest we need sometimes, but you could take a look at these examples and go with what sounds best to you at this moment.

1. Physical: sleep, lying or sitting down, yoga, stretching or going on a gentle walk

2. Mental: Journalling or taking time to daydream

3. Sensory: Taking screen-free time, turning down lights, wearing noise-cancelling headphones or mindfully using your senses to notice five things around you

4. Emotional: Spending time with trusted family members and friends, talking about your worries or problems

5. Social: Depending on how you're feeling and what recharges you, either seeking out the company of others or spending some time alone

6. Creative: Giving yourself a break from a project or problem, or spending time in inspiring settings (maybe in nature, an art gallery or a bookshop), without putting pressure on yourself to create

7. Spiritual: Connecting to something bigger than yourself by volunteering in your community, mindful walking and meditation (see page 174), or prayer

Brain science

Many experts have shown that spending time in nature can have wonderfully positive effects on humans' physical and **mental health**. One found that a 15-minute walk in nature (perhaps along a river, in a wood or around a local park) had effects that a city walk didn't. Some scientists also believe that time in nature can help reduce ADHD **symptoms**, including a restless mind.

Handling hyperactivity

Physical hyperactivity

Sometimes you don't need a rest exactly; you just want to make your **hyperactivity** feel less uncomfortable. Allowing yourself to fidget, perhaps with aids such as fidget toys or rocking footrests, could be helpful. This is also known as **stimming**.

You can read more about stimming in the Loris chapter (see pages 171–172).

You could also try taking regular movement breaks (standing up and walking around, for example) during times when you're asked to stay mostly still.

If teachers and others aren't already understanding of your additional movement needs, ask a trusted adult to talk to them. Help them understand that fidgeting and/or moving more actually helps you concentrate, and that the discomfort (and potentially pain) that you feel when you can't do this is distracting as well as unpleasant.

Mental hyperactivity

If it's your brain that's distractingly busy, you may find yourself feeling mentally **overwhelmed**, almost like you're 'spinning in circles' inside your mind.

You could try releasing some of these thoughts with a **brain dump**, either scribbling down your thoughts or recording yourself talking. It might then help to organise these thoughts, pulling out anything that is urgent, important or that is particularly bothering you.

It can really help to talk things through as you do this, and you might also find mind maps and bullet-point lists to be useful tools.

Remember that you deserve to have your needs supported, and shouldn't have to pretend everything's OK. If you feel safe doing it, you can try being more open with people when your physical or mental **hyperactivity** is distracting you. For example, if you're finding it tricky to listen to a friend while sitting still because you feel so restless, you could ask them if you could walk and talk together instead.

Brain break
Facts, games and ADHD-friendly activities to give your brain a rest

Bees have a number of super senses that help them find their way from flower to flower! They can see **ultraviolet (UV)** light, which reveals 'nectar guide' patterns on flower petals. These are invisible to humans, but show insects exactly where to land.

Bees also seem to use Earth's magnetic field and the position of the Sun to find their way around. They can also apparently sense the weak electricity in the air surrounding a flower, and even tell if another bee has recently visited it!

I heard screen time causes ADHD. Why can't you just stop using screens?

There doesn't seem to be any clear evidence that ADHD is caused by screen time of any kind – TV, computer, phone, tablet or any other device.

However, some scientists have found a possible link between higher levels of screen time and issues with attention and **impulsivity**, which are similar to (but not the same as) certain ADHD symptoms. These results have sometimes been misreported as screen time causing ADHD.

We still need more research to understand the effects of screen time on our brains, especially using digital devices for multiple hours every day. It may be that not all screen time has the same effect, or that the problem is more about what we're missing out on when we're staring at a screen (such as active hobbies or face-to-face communication).

The Māori term for ADHD is *aroreretini*, which means 'attention goes to many things'. This was one of many new, deliberately non-judgemental and strength-focused words added to the Māori language in 2017 to discuss disability, **mental health** and addiction.

Side quest

Think of a random place, animal and object, and write them down. Set a timer for two minutes and make up a story about all three. You can record yourself speaking it aloud, instead of writing, if you want. Don't worry about whether it's good — just have fun!

Chapter four
Tortoise

Tortoise
Making slow progress

Struggle

A tortoise is an impressive animal for all sorts of reasons – from its tough, beautiful shell to its outrageously long lifespan. However, speed is not exactly its strong suit. On average, a tortoise seems to take around 3 hours to travel one kilometre. A human can typically walk this far in 10–12 minutes, and a cheetah at top speed would be able to run it in 30 seconds flat!

Sometimes, it can feel like we're taking ages to get things done or learn new information and skills. It can be pretty disheartening, especially when we're trying really hard but others still seem to be zipping ahead of us, making it all look so easy and effortless!

There is evidence that people with ADHD can sometimes take longer to process information. Sometimes, this may be due to slow processing speed (SPS). This is when the brain needs a bit more time to take in, make sense of, and respond to information. Many people with ADHD seem to have SPS, but it isn't an ADHD **symptom** and people without ADHD can have it, too. Processing speed isn't the same as intelligence, and SPS doesn't limit what someone can understand and learn – it just means that it can take a bit longer.

Brain science

Messages in the brain are carried along fibres, like TV cables, made of long cells called **neurons**. When we grow up, these fibres become coated with a fatty substance called myelin. Although scientists aren't entirely sure what causes slow processing speed, it has been suggested that a thinner myelin coating may make these fibres slower when they are carrying messages.

Various ADHD **traits** could also play a part in slowing down our progress. For example, we may get distracted by our own **hyperactivity** or wandering thoughts, meaning that we're not really taking in the information that we want to focus on. Memory differences might also make us forget what we've already learned, even if we covered it very recently, so we may need to go over it several times.

Strength

Remember the story of 'The Tortoise and the Hare'? Spoiler: the slow-moving tortoise doesn't give up, and ends up beating the speedy but overconfident hare who's not bothering to try! Real-life tortoises may not be fast but they are determined — even though they travel at only 0.2 miles per hour, escaped pet tortoises are often found several miles from home! And guess what? They've been doing all this for over 200 million years. That's right, tortoises were plodding along back when dinosaurs roamed the Earth, proving that slow and steady really *does* win the race.

It can be tough when we feel like we're working so hard and others are still flying ahead of us. But it's amazing how much progress we can make, even going more slowly, when we don't give up. People with ADHD often experience time as either 'now' or 'not now', rather than the more ordered **neurotypical** sense of time stretching from now into the future in equal, dependable hours and days. So we may need support to really imagine, or believe, that the results of our effort are building up – little by little – over time.

We're also developing valuable skills, such as perseverance – the ability to keep trying even when things are difficult and taking a long time. And we're learning how to *learn* – how to get our head around things that, at times, feel beyond our understanding. This is an incredibly useful skill to develop as we grow older, and the things we need to do and learn become more and more complicated.

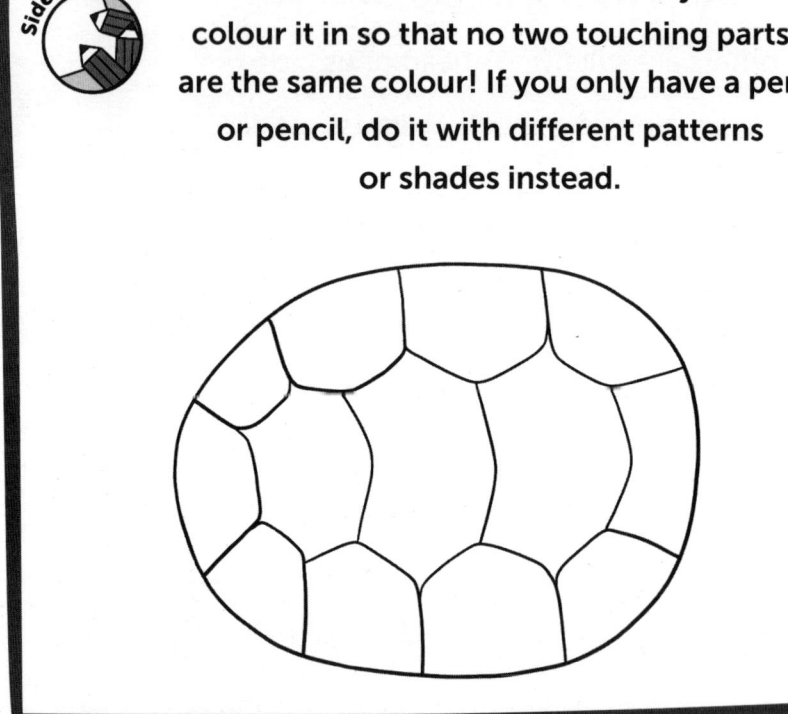

Side quest

Trace this tortoise shell and try to colour it in so that no two touching parts are the same colour! If you only have a pen or pencil, do it with different patterns or shades instead.

Working with your brain

It can be so discouraging when things feel like they take longer for you, no matter how hard you're trying — particularly when your **dopamine**-seeking brain wants to move onto something else quickly. This means that it's really important to show yourself some **compassion**. Self-compassion is something that **ADHDers** can often find challenging — you can find some ideas for building this on pages 244–248.

ADHD often co-occurs with (exists alongside) other conditions — such as **dyslexia, dyscalculia, dyspraxia** and **auditory processing disorder**. This can also make learning take longer and feel more challenging. If you're finding reading, writing, maths, understanding people when they talk, or anything else particularly difficult, it's worth talking to a trusted adult. Together, you can decide if you would like to meet with a medical professional, either for advice or to find out if you have a co-occurring condition.

Making progress

Try to remember that, although things may be happening a bit more slowly, they are still happening! **ADHDers** don't always notice this ourselves because of the different way our brains tend to understand time (see page 26). To help give yourself a sense of this progress, you can ask a trusted adult to check in regularly when you're working on a school project or tricky topic, developing a new skill or doing something else that can't be finished in one go.

It can be helpful to track this visually. Imagining your project like a race, try drawing a 'start to finish' line towards your goal with progress points along the way, and see how far you are on this line. You could use colours, stickers, draw funny characters — anything that makes it more fun! Even if you haven't made as much progress as you like, you can talk through what you are learning and what skills you are practising along the way — including perseverance. It's also a chance to talk about anything that you might be stuck on, and to think about any extra support you might need.

Regular progress check-ins can break up what might feel like a long, slow slog into more manageable steps. Try scheduling them in, ideally with a trusted adult, at a set time once a week – they only need to take a minute! Make sure to celebrate your efforts and your progress along the way, too. This can give you a confidence boost and sense of achievement that provides your brain with a very welcome dose of **dopamine**. If your brain recognises what you're doing as a good source of dopamine, this may make it easier to stick with it.

Over and over

Everyone tends to forget things they've learned over a certain length of time. But for **ADHDers**, our memory differences can slow things down as we try to retain information, build on what we've learned and confidently move on to more advanced work.

A technique called spaced repetitions can help with remembering information. It trains your brain like a muscle, strengthening its ability to fetch a piece of information.

In spaced repetitions, you repeatedly go back and review information you've learned. With each successful review, you gradually widen the gap of time between repetitions, which helps your brain move the information from your short-term memory into long-term memory storage. This could be your repetition schedule:

My repetition schedule

1. Same day
2. Next day
3. Three days later
4. One week later

I know people who really like this method. However, personally, this schedule feels really **overwhelming** to me. I find it hard to think about juggling this for all the different things I'm trying to remember! How do you feel about it? You don't have to do things perfectly for them to have an impact – you can do them in the way that works for you. There is no one right way for everyone with ADHD, so why not give it a go if you think it might work for you?

Another way to check what you're taking in could be by creating a 'start to finish line' (see page 76) for the subject you're finding tricky and draw 'memory checkpoints' along it. When you reach a checkpoint, your trusted adult could quiz you on what you've learned. Don't worry about getting everything right – just give it a go, and note down anything you find tricky so that you know what to focus on practising. You could even try teaching your trusted adult what you've learned – this is a great way to make sure you understand and remember the most important points.

Brain and body boosts

When things feel like they're taking a long time, we can get bored or feel understimulated (like not enough is happening), which can affect our concentration and slow our progress. **ADHDers** may feel exhausted (to the point of actually falling asleep) and irritable, and even have physical effects such as shooting pains in our legs (I absolutely get these!) We might also distract ourselves from the reality of a situation we don't want to be in, disappearing into the wandering thoughts in our mind.

Perseverance is a brilliant skill to learn, but it can sometimes involve letting ourselves feel uncomfortable. A little bit of discomfort is OK sometimes, but not to the point where you keep going despite being in pain or distress. It's not only unkind to ourselves, it's unhelpful too, because it means we're not in the right frame of mind to learn. This can make whatever we're trying to do even harder to slog through, and be so unpleasant that our brain, in its attempt to protect us, tries to avoid ever having to do it again!

When things feel slow and understimulating, physical movement may help give you a little boost to keep going. You could take a break and walk around a bit, or **stim** (see pages 171–172) while you stay in your seat – maybe by playing with a fidget toy or using a rocking footrest. Music or background TV (that isn't too attention-grabbing – maybe a show or video you've seen lots of times before) may also help to keep you engaged.

You can also give your brain little **dopamine** boosts, to try to wake it up and keep it happy, by breaking down your task into smaller steps that you can tick off – or give yourself stars and stickers for! I and many other adults with ADHD still use colourful, shiny, cartoony or otherwise fun 'props' – from reward stickers to patterned pens – to help keep our brains happier while we work!

Brain break
Facts, games and ADHD-friendly activities to give your brain a rest

Did you know that tortoises are some of the longest-living animals on Earth? A Seychelles giant tortoise called Jonathan holds the record as the oldest-known land animal, believed to be over 190 years old. He was born before the telephone, postage stamp or lightbulb were invented!

 **Follow these five simple steps to draw your own tortoise.**

1. Draw the top part of the shell.

2. Add the head and neck, and the bottom part of the shell.

3. Add two legs ...

4. ... and then two more!

5. Draw in the shell pattern, and add in a friendly face and some little claws.

IRRITATING ADHD QUESTIONS:

You seem smart – why do you need extra help?

ADHD doesn't affect how intelligent someone is – it affects how their brain works when it comes to concentration, organisation and managing time. So even if someone is very skilled and knowledgeable in certain areas, that doesn't necessarily mean that they find it easy to finish tasks, remember instructions or stay on track.

Extra help can give people the right tools to work with their unique brain. Just like glasses help people see clearly, support can help people with ADHD learn clearly.

Side quest

The Half Tortoise is a yoga pose that helps relax the body and give the spine a nice stretch. If you'd like to try it, start by kneeling and then sitting back on your heels. Then lift your arms up and stretch them forward towards the floor, bringing your head down gradually, too. Only go as far as is comfortable! Take a couple of deep breaths, if the pose feels OK, and then gently return to your starting position.

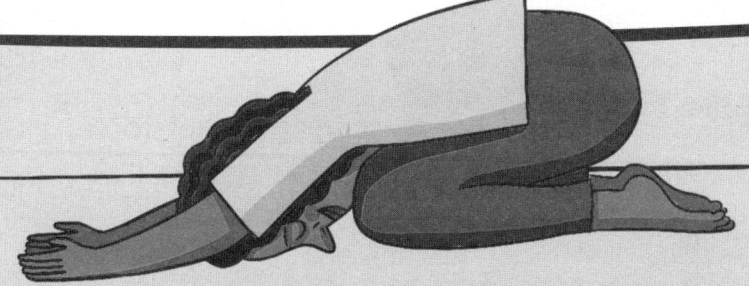

Did you know?

Did you know that whether a tortoise is born a boy or a girl depends on how warm the weather is when the baby tortoise is still inside the egg? Warmer eggs usually hatch girls, cooler eggs hatch boys!

Chapter five
Salmon

Salmon
Leaping into new challenges

Struggle

One day, a salmon is happily swimming around in the ocean, feasting on all sorts of food and growing big and strong. Then, suddenly, a powerful impulse takes over, urging the fish to travel back to the stream where it hatched in order to breed there. Its journey may be thousands of miles long, fighting against fast-moving currents and even leaping up huge waterfalls along the way!

There's lots more about many ADHDers' attraction to new things in the Magpie chapter on page 17.

People with ADHD might find it easier than most to imagine an impulse so strong that it pushes you to take on a huge challenge like this. **Impulsivity** is a core **trait** of ADHD so it can be much more difficult for us to stop, think and possibly reject an impulse rather than just go with the flow. This means we can find exciting new interests, ideas and plans irresistible, even when we have a lot – maybe too much – going on already.

Brain science

ADHDers' higher levels of impulsivity may be caused, at least partly, by differences in how the prefrontal cortex, the part of our brain underneath the forehead, communicates with some deep brain regions called the basal ganglia and the thalamus. These work as a sort of 'gate', sending signals to allow behaviours either to go ahead (open gate) or stop (shut gate). For those with ADHD, this gate tends to be 'stuck open', so to speak, so it doesn't automatically stop impulses before our conscious thoughts kick in. This may happen only after the action.

Being **impulsive** can also mean that **ADHDers** may start a new project without thinking how much time it will take. Many of us also experience something known as time agnosia, a difference in how accurately we sense time passing. This can mean that we may take on big projects or challenges, or try to pack even more new activities into our busy days, without really understanding how much more time and energy this will demand of us. Trying to do too much, even if it's things we're really passionate about, can mean that – like a salmon trying to leap up too many big waterfalls – we get too exhausted to carry on!

Overloading our days, without giving our brains and bodies enough rest, can make life feel **overwhelming**, stressful and unmanageable at times, eventually leading to **burnout**. Not fun! However, it can be really tempting to keep filling our lives with more interest, more excitement – just more, more, more!

Learn more about time agnosia on page 26 and about ADHD burnout on page 56.

From crossing the road without looking properly to snapping at people, impulsive behaviour can sometimes be unhelpful or even dangerous. Talk to a trusted adult about developing strategies to help keep you safe and prevent misunderstandings. For instance, you could practise stopping and counting to five as you look both ways before crossing the road. Make sure to keep up these strategies so that they eventually become a habit.

Strength

The ADHD tendency towards impulsivity – acting before we fully think through or plan things – can sometimes lead us into tricky situations. But it can also help to fill our lives with excitement, joy and meaning, and lead us to achieve amazing, possibly world-changing things!

The strength of our inner pull to take on new challenges, explore new ideas and try new activities may help make us more **spontaneous**. Rather than wanting to do something for months or years, but never quite taking the plunge, this impulsive drive can launch us into action before we have a chance to talk ourselves out of it.

Many **ADHDers** seem to experience time in a less structured way than **neurotypical** people do, largely divided into 'now' and 'not now' rather than neat, even portions of past, present and future time. If something doesn't happen now, our brains might not trust that it will happen at all. So while many people delay doing joyful or meaningful things, promising themselves they'll do them later and never actually getting round to them, we may follow our impulse to do these things right away! As a result, we might end up having all kinds of fun, life-enriching experiences rather than missing the opportunity and regretting it later on.

Sometimes, acting from impulse rather than cautious logic can also open up possibilities that others may have dismissed as too difficult, or too different from 'how things are done'. Like a salmon's instinct powering it through a seemingly impossible journey upstream, our gut feeling may help push us straight through those 'typical' limits that others put on themselves.

Of course, many salmon don't reach their final goal – but millions do! Although not all our ambitious ideas and plans will succeed, we'll learn from our efforts – and we might just do something incredible. There are many wildly successful people with ADHD, including record-breaking Olympic athletes, top Hollywood directors, legendary musicians and owners of world-famous businesses. When ADHDers find something that we love and care about, and put our effort and enthusiasm into it, we can achieve great things!

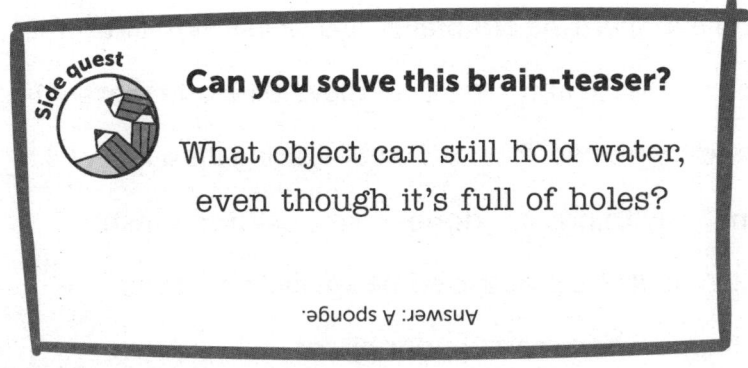

Side quest

Can you solve this brain-teaser?

What object can still hold water, even though it's full of holes?

Answer: A sponge.

Working with your brain

ADHDers don't need to squash our wonderfully creative, curious and joyful impulses to do new things. Experts have shown that our **impulsivity** can actually make our lives feel richer, happier and more **fulfilled**.

However, trying to do too much can end up leaving us so stressed and tired that we can't enjoy any of it, and risk damaging our physical and **mental health**. It can also mean that we don't make much progress with anything we're doing, which can feel disheartening.

At the same time, we might not want to give up anything either, as some people with ADHD tend to **prioritise** tasks differently to **neurotypical** people. Our brains may see all things as equally important, so we don't choose between them. As our brains also tend to imagine time in terms of 'now' and 'not now', they can worry that putting something aside 'for now' means giving it up forever!

It can really help to use some special strategies to support and reassure our brains.

→ Try writing a list of everything that you're trying to do at the moment. For example, you could note down sleep, meals, schoolwork, chores, clubs, hobbies, and plans with friends and family.

If you have a weekly schedule written down (see the Scaffolding section on page 249), you can check this for activities.

→ If you have any new ideas for things you really want to do, even if you don't think you'll have the time or energy for them at the moment, add these below the list.

→ Ask a trusted adult to check the list with you to make sure it includes everything. Talk through which things you have to do and which things you want to do, marking them with different-coloured pens.

→ Is there anything on the list that you could happily stop doing? If not, is there anything you would feel OK about pausing? Remind your brain that this won't be forever by writing down a particular date when things should be calmer and you can pick up the activity again.

→ Ask your trusted adult to help you work out how long each thing on the list takes. Include time to prepare for activities, travel and rest afterwards. Check these times against your weekly schedule, if you have one – I'd suggest making one if not!

→ Is fitting everything in a squeeze? If so, think about pausing at least one more thing. We can often underestimate how long things take, so it's good to leave free time.

→ Try to leave extra free time for being **spontaneous**, allowing yourself to follow some fun, creative impulses as they come up!

My list

- Sleep enough each night
- Eat regular meals
- Do my schoolwork
- Help with chores at home
- Go to clubs or after-school activities
- Make time for hobbies I enjoy
- Try something fun or creative this week!

It can be empowering to remember that **ADHDers** can and do achieve great, world-changing things. Some of our common **traits** and tendencies – such as **impulsivity**, creativity and eagerness – may actually help us to do this.

We still have to work extra hard in other ways, though, to help our brains with remembering things, starting tasks and more. We also need to be aware of our basic needs and energy levels, and to remember that no achievement is more important than taking care of ourselves.

You don't need to be exceptional or do as much as humanly possible just to prove your worth. You're wonderful just as you are, and your goals and dreams are for enriching your life – not justifying it.

Many people struggle to show themselves kindness and understanding, whether they have ADHD or not. Find out how to develop your self-compassion on pages 244–248.

Brain break

Facts, games and ADHD-friendly activities to give your brain a rest

Did you know?

Salmon and flamingos get their famous pink colour the same way: they both eat tiny creatures that contain a substance called astaxanthin. Without astaxanthin, salmon flesh and flamingo feathers would be white or grey. Farmed salmon and flamingos in zoos have astaxanthin mixed into their food so they stay pink!

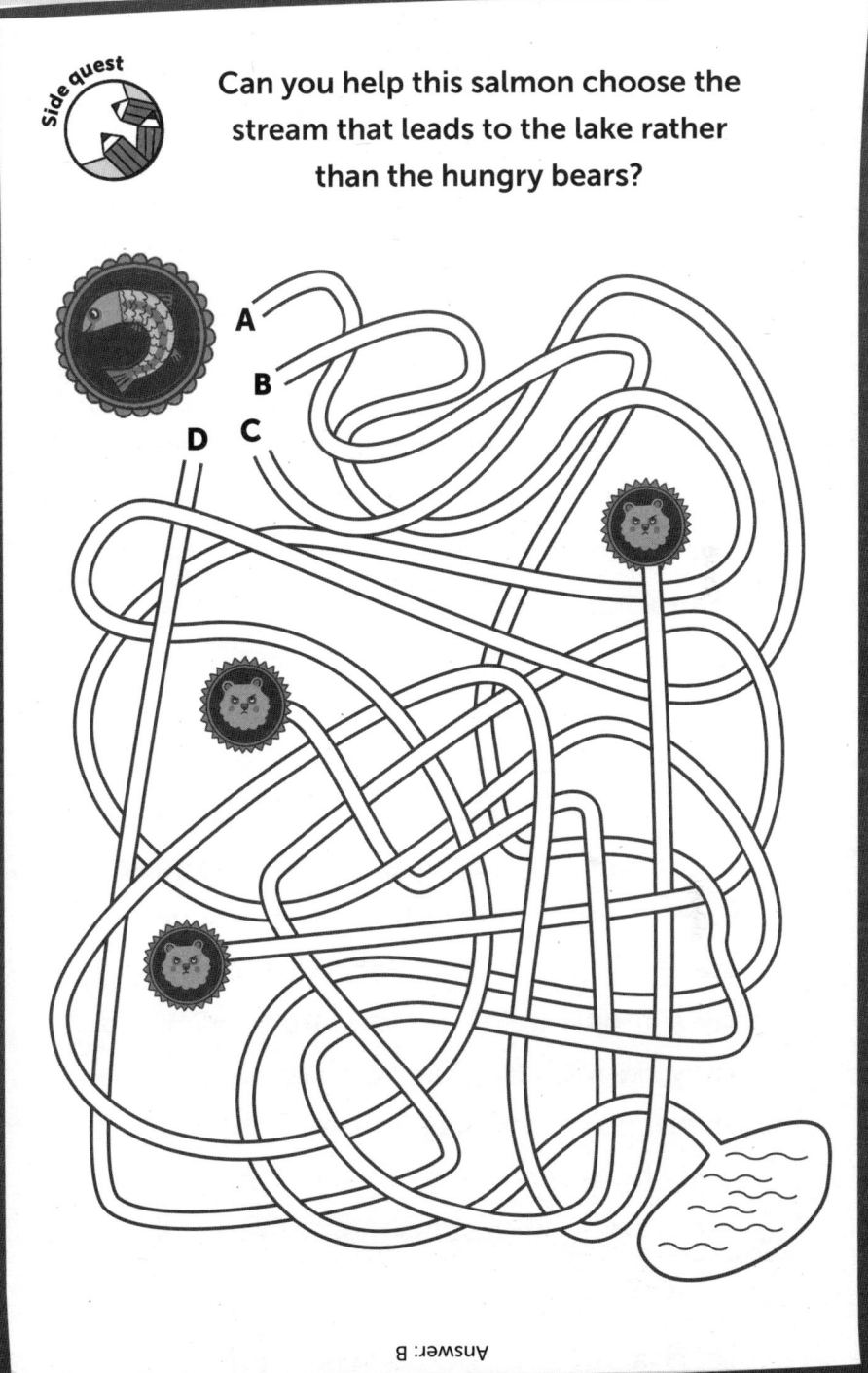

Side quest

Can you help this salmon choose the stream that leads to the lake rather than the hungry bears?

A
B
C
D

Answer: B

IRRITATING ADHD QUESTIONS:

> You can't have ADHD if you're doing well at school, can you?

Yes, you can! ADHD **traits** can make school more challenging, especially when our needs aren't properly supported. However, it's absolutely possible to have ADHD and also get high marks and positive school reports.

Many young people actually miss out on **diagnosis** and support because they don't fit the image many people have of someone with ADHD. For example, they stay still and quiet in class. These ADHDers may be **masking** their differences – for example, managing to get high marks only by working all night to 'catch up' and exhausting themselves.

Some scientists have suggested that the ADHD tendency to explore may have been an evolutionary advantage for early **hunter-gatherers**. In a 2014 study, people had to click on berry bushes on a screen to gather as many berries as possible within a time limit.

People with ADHD traits moved to new bushes sooner than those without, despite this taking up precious time. Moving sooner meant they avoided over-picking the bushes, and gathered more berries overall!

Did you know?

Atlantic salmon can go without food for six months as they migrate upstream. They typically don't eat once they enter fresh water on their migration, and only start again once they've returned to the salty sea — if they survive!

Chapter six
Parrot

Parrot
Chatting a lot

Strength

Have you ever seen videos online of pet parrots talking away to their owners? Millions of people love watching these charming chatterboxes coming out with all sorts of funny, surprising and often very sweet things. African grey parrots are particularly big talkers, with some able to learn hundreds of different words!

ADHDers are all different, of course, but chattiness is something that a lot of us have in common. We often bring lots of energy and interest to a conversation, which can make us really fun and exciting to be around!

Our chattiness can help avoid awkward silences, and create a friendly and welcoming atmosphere for others. We may enjoy chatting away, too, as a way of sharing our ideas and interests, and to connect with people.

Our lower levels of impulse control can mean that we don't 'filter' ourselves as much in conversation. That is, we often speak before we've thought through what we're going to say, and without adapting it to what others may want to hear. Although this can sometimes cause issues, it can also mean that we come across as refreshingly open and honest.

Impulsiveness is explored more in the Salmon chapter on page 87.

Showing people our true selves in this way may help put them at ease. They can relax and be themselves too, instead of hiding their real thoughts, unique quirks and strong emotions. That's where real human connections can be made and deepened: in surprising and meaningful moments, rather than when everyone's just going through the motions of conversation.

Side quest

Can you unmuddle the words below to get the name of an animal?

ONE SAIL

Answer: Sea lion

Struggle

Being chatty can often be great fun, for us and for others, and can really help us to form close connections. At other times though, this talkative tendency can cause us problems. We may not notice quite how much we're talking and how others are reacting to it — or we might notice but still feel unable to stop. We can also sometimes blurt things out, before we've had time to think about how others might react to them.

Sometimes, **ADHDers** can be so excited to chat that we accidentally don't leave space for whoever we're speaking to. We may interrupt people, not ask many questions or not leave silences for others to speak. This can make our well-meaning sharing of our thoughts, feelings, stories and other things we find interesting seem like we're trying to make the conversation all about us. It's the exact opposite of what we're typically trying to do when chatting: connect with others.

The ADHD brain's tendency towards both **impulsivity** and **working memory** differences help explain why we often interrupt others. We feel unable to hold back what we have to say until someone else has finished talking. We could worry about getting a thought out before it disappears from our mind, quite possibly forever. Memory differences could also mean that we forget what a conversation was originally about, especially if we've jumped in with a thought that has led us somewhere different.

Many people can feel uncomfortable talking about personal, emotional or **controversial** subjects unless they know each other very well. They may prefer talking about things that feel safer and less sensitive (like the weather or traffic), and could find some of our more impulse-led, unfiltered approaches too **overwhelming**. Some people can also find lots of talking hard to keep up with – especially if it's fast, includes lots of detail and jumps around between different subjects.

These are differences in communication, not things that are 'wrong' with **ADHDers**. However, negative responses may make us feel embarrassed or even threatened. This reaction may be more extreme for some of us, especially if we experience **rejection sensitivity**.

You can find out more about rejection sensitivity in the Elephant chapter (page 127).

It is important to keep yourself safe by not oversharing (by giving out personal details and so on) both online and offline.

Working with your brain

There is no one right way to have a conversation, no matter what society's unspoken 'rules' may say. Judgemental terms such as 'excessive talking', 'over-sharing' and 'over-explaining' may make it seem as if there are set standards for how much we should talk, what we should talk about and how much detail we should include. But who gets to decide what these standards are? And who says that's what everyone wants?

I love when people commit supposed 'conversational crimes' and respond to (or even excitedly interrupt) me with an idea of their own. I don't find it self-centred or competitive, as some people apparently do. I see it as them being **empathetic**, engaged and generous, trying to connect with me by sharing something of their own. I also don't care if people talk quickly or loudly, or if our conversation jumps around, dropping threads and picking them up (or not) later on. From talking to other people, particularly those in ADHD communities, I know I'm not alone in feeling this way!

Masking

Masking is when people hide their differences from others – either on purpose or without realising – to seem more **neurotypical**.

For instance, some **ADHDers** are naturally very chatty, but feel so worried and self-conscious about accidentally upsetting people or pushing them away that we mask in most conversations. This might involve keeping quiet most of the time, hiding our emotions and real opinions, cutting ourselves off after just a few words or only ever talking about light subjects that we're sure are appropriate.

This is so understandable, but so sad. In trying to avoid negative feedback from others, and painful feelings of embarrassment and shame, we are also denying ourselves joy, self-expression and the human connection that comes from letting others see our true selves. This could leave us feeling isolated, negatively affecting our friendships and also our

mental health. The effort of constantly masking may also be exhausting, potentially leading to ADHD **burnout** (see page 56).

Chatty check-ins

People approach and enjoy conversations in all sorts of different ways, and no one is 'wrong' for that. Chatty ADHDers (like me!) can work on our self-awareness and practise making space for others in conversations, while also refusing to feel ashamed of the way we are. Here are three points that it could be helpful to think about:

1. Questions: I always used to assume that other people were like me and that if they wanted to say something, they'd just jump in and say it! This is true for some people, but over time, I've discovered that others can find it tricky to do this and may prefer to be 'invited' to talk through direct questions.

A simple 'What do you think?' or 'How do you feel about that?' can be a great way to hear what people have to say and develop a stronger connection with them. So can asking someone the same question that they've just asked you, once you've finished answering it yourself, or asking them a follow-up question when they do tell you something.

Don't worry or feel down on yourself if you realise that you've forgotten to ask many (or any) questions – it's easily done! And if there was something specific or important that you meant to ask someone about – for example, checking in on a problem they told you about, asking about a shared project or congratulating them on exciting news – but you forgot and they didn't bring it up, you could write yourself a reminder (see the Scaffolding section on page 249) to do this next time you see them.

2. Interruptions: If I recorded conversations with my closest friends, I'm sure I'd find that we almost never finish a sentence because we're constantly interrupting each other! I love this kind of excited, joyfully chaotic, overlapping chat, but I've also learned that other people can find interruptions really difficult – and that's OK, too.

The more interested I am in what someone is saying and the more comfortable I feel in the conversation, the more likely I am to interrupt them. For me, an interruption means 'Yes, I'm so engaged that I can guess where you're going, and I'm so excited to share something back that I can't wait for you to finish – especially because I worry I'll forget my thought if I do!' However, I've learned that people can assume that interrupting them means I'm not interested in what they're saying. It's not my fault, or theirs – just a difference.

Similarly, others may not want to interrupt us while we're talking, so if we're waiting for them to jump in, we might find ourselves waffling on for a long time! If you notice that the other person hasn't spoken for a while, and you're feeling worried that the conversation has accidentally become a bit one-sided, you could try stopping and taking a deep breath to see if they use the moment of silence to respond. If you do interrupt, you can always catch yourself and say something like 'Sorry, I cut you off!' or 'Sorry, please carry on!' to the person you interrupted. If you feel comfortable doing so, you can also let people know that your ADHD might mean you communicate a bit differently to them, and maybe share what this means for you.

3. Timing: When you're bursting to say something, it can feel quite uncomfortable to keep it in! In situations where chattiness isn't really appropriate – like doing tests in class, watching a movie at the cinema, or quiet reading time – you can try noting down your thoughts if they feel important. At other times, people may not seem like they want to talk, even when the timing feels fine. Chatty **ADHDers** can sometimes take this to heart, and may even experience **rejection sensitivity** (see page 127), but it's important to remember that there

are many possible reasons for this that have nothing to do with you – including that person just needing some quiet time. You're not a mind-reader, and you're not responsible for everyone else's moods and feelings, so try not to put this on yourself!

Unmasking

Unmasking is when **neurodivergent** people, such as ADHDers, feel safe and confident enough to let our guard down and stop hiding our differences. Although the three points we've just looked at can help make conversations go more smoothly, whether they're with new people or close friends, it's more important to find people who we feel comfortable unmasking with.

If someone we think is a friend makes us feel upset, uncomfortable, or even that we're being judged when we talk to them, are they actually a good fit for us? There will be people who love how chatty and excitable we are, and how varied, deep and fact-packed our conversations can be. They will appreciate our (sometimes imperfect) efforts to make sure they feel valued and included. These are the people worth taking time to build and maintain friendships with!

As well as developing strong friendships and positive relationships with **neurotypical** people, it can also be really healing (and fun!) to spend time in **neurodivergent** spaces. You may feel safer to **unmask** and be yourself, knowing that you're not being judged for any of the things you might normally worry about, including missing neurotypical **social cues**. If you interrupt, for instance, people should understand that it's a common ADHD thing, and know you don't mean anything by it!

Try finding a nearby group for people who are neurodivergent and your age. If there isn't one, you could ask a trusted adult to help you start one at your school or in your local area.

Brain break
Facts, games and ADHD-friendly activities to give your brain a rest

The African grey parrot is one of the most intelligent birds in the world. Experts believe it is as clever as an average five-year-old child! In 2020, an African grey parrot named Griffin performed as well as a group of university students on 12 out of 14 intelligence tests.

Try this word game with a friend or family member, or challenge yourself! See how many synonyms (words with the same or similar meanings) you can come up with for each of these words:

Nice   Smelly   New

You've got good parents – how can you have ADHD?

ADHD is definitely not caused by 'bad' parenting. It tends to run in families because it is strongly genetic, meaning that it often passes from parents to children.

There does seem to be an association between ADHD and **traumatic** events in childhood, such as divorce, abuse or witnessing violence. However, understanding these links is very complex. Experts still aren't clear on how different situations might affect the development of ADHD.

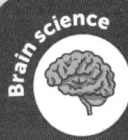

Many people have suggested that ADHD (Attention Deficit Hyperactivity Disorder) should be renamed. Some think that the '**hyperactivity**' part is misleading, as it doesn't apply to all types of ADHD. Another complaint is that **ADHDers** don't really have a 'deficit' (lack) of attention, as we can sometimes focus well — or even **hyperfocus** (see the Cheetah chapter on page 179). Some believe that a word like 'variable' (different) would be more appropriate.

Some new ideas for names include 'Attention Variability Disorder', 'Self-Regulation Deficit Disorder' and '**Executive Function** Deficit Disorder'. With a trusted adult, try looking up what all their technical-sounding words mean. Do any of them fit well with your experiences? Can you come up with a better name?

Many people don't like their **neurodivergence** being described as a 'disorder' — one alternative suggestion is 'Attention Distribution and Hyperactivity Difference'. What do you think?

Chapter seven
Elephant

Elephant
Feeling super-sensitive

Strength

Elephants are one of the most intelligent animals on Earth and multiple studies have found that they are highly sensitive, emotional and **empathetic** creatures. They have been seen caring for ill members of their herd by stroking or feeding them. They even appear to cry when rejected and to mourn their dead.

People with ADHD often report being very sensitive, in a number of different ways. One of these is what is known as **justice sensitivity**.

Justice sensitivity is a tendency to have a strong sense of right and wrong, and not be able to just ignore or accept when something seems unfair, like many people do. Some studies have found that people with ADHD and some **autistic** people tend to have higher levels of justice sensitivity than **neurotypical** people. Other studies suggest that there is also a link between higher

impulsivity and higher levels of altruism, which is the tendency to help others without expecting anything in return.

All of this could explain why, in another study, people with ADHD were more likely to show kindness to others when there was no clear reward. Researchers have also found that **ADHDers** are more likely to try and restore justice when a situation feels unfair – even if this hurts us in the long term.

Brain science

Empathy is an important skill that lets us imagine what it would be like to be in someone else's situation. Using empathy can resolve arguments more positively, build stronger relationships and reach more people to join causes that are important to us.

Standing up for ourselves is brave and important, and having such a strong sense of **empathy** and fairness that we stand up for others (even when it may affect us negatively) is a powerful thing. This is true whether it relates to a friend or classmate, a **marginalised** or **persecuted** group, or even the environment.

Sometimes, this deep-rooted sense of justice can be seen by others as questioning **authority** or challenging both unwritten and established 'rules' that we all live by. But while many rules exist for a good reason, history has taught us over and over how important it is to not just mindlessly accept rules that hurt people and our planet. A strong internal sense of justice is what

has brought about all kinds of positive progress, from women's right to vote and the **Civil Rights movement** to **LGBTQIA+** rights and climate action.

Struggle

Elephants can often be as strong-willed as they are sensitive, getting very upset by forced changes or apparent threats. Elephants have been known to break down electric fences and stomp across busy roads – or even through towns – rather than abandon their favoured routes to food, water and meeting points.

Although **ADHDers** aren't tearing apart towns(!), the way we handle big feelings, as well as strong impulses, can look different for us. Our moods may swing from high to low, quickly and intensely. Some experts have suggested that these differences in managing emotions – known as emotional dysregulation – may be a core **symptom** of ADHD, alongside attention differences, **hyperactivity** and **impulsivity**.

Emotional dysregulation may combine with our **justice sensitivity**, meaning that we can become angry and distressed more easily when a rule or decision feels unjust, or someone is behaving in a way that seems unfair or morally wrong. An ADHD tendency to be more **impulsive** might make us more likely to act on our feelings, too (see the Salmon chapter on page 87). Although this can sometimes be a good thing, there are also times where it could be unhelpful or even dangerous in the moment.

Brain science

Experts believe that up to 65 per cent of people with ADHD may also have something called 'Oppositional Defiant Disorder' (ODD). People with ODD often feel resentful towards **authority** figures, like parents or teachers, and refuse to do what they say. Unlike justice sensitivity, ODD is a condition that is linked to other patterns of behaviour, such as constant feelings of anger and challenges with social skills.

Rejection sensitivity

Although it is not an officially recognised **symptom** of ADHD, many **ADHDers** also talk about experiencing **rejection sensitivity**. This describes feeling so upset by rejection or criticism – whether real or imagined – that we feel **overwhelmingly** intense emotional pain. Of course, no one likes feeling rejected, but this is a particularly strong sensitivity to situations that many people wouldn't worry about. For example, thinking a friend must hate us if they don't come over to talk to us right away, or worrying that if our football coach asks to speak to us, it's because they're about to kick us off the team.

Evidence suggests that experiencing rejection sensitivity can **trigger** changes in the body, including a fight-flight-or-freeze response to danger (see page 128). Rejection sensitivity can be so distressing that it can cause people to avoid situations that might trigger this reaction. This may mean withdrawing from friendships, school, favourite hobbies and more. It could also mean **masking** or constantly second-guessing what people are thinking to avoid negative reactions.

Ever heard of 'fight, flight or freeze'? When we experience something that feels dangerous or very stressful, one part of our brain — the **amygdala** — sends a distress signal to another part of our brain called the hypothalamus.

The hypothalamus sends messages out to the rest of our body, through our **nervous system**, to react quickly to protect us — often either by fighting back, running away or freezing on the spot. Although this response can be life-saving when we're in serious danger, it can be hard on our bodies if it is repeatedly **triggered** by stress.

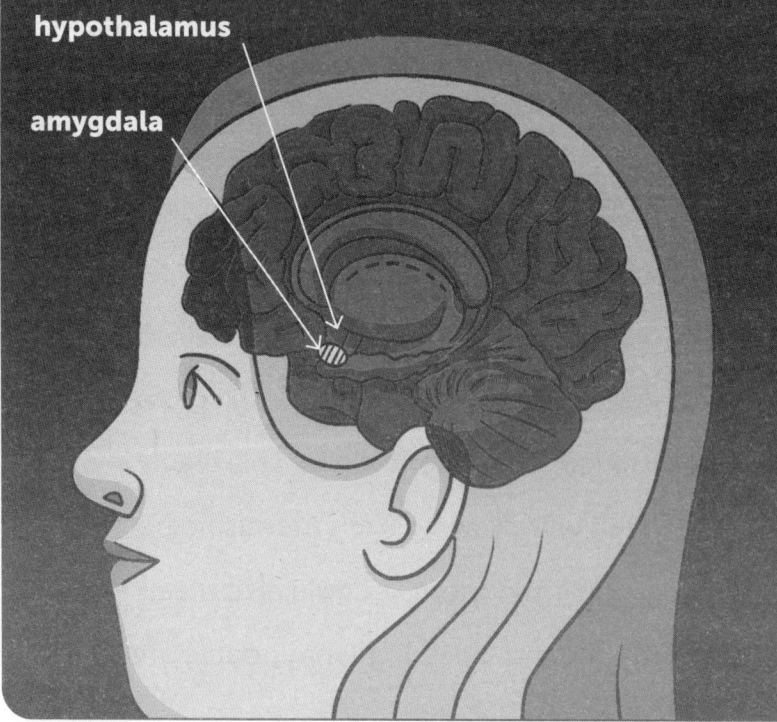

hypothalamus

amygdala

Experts think that **ADHDers'** higher levels of **justice sensitivity** may be due in part to a tendency towards cognitive rigidity – resistance to changing beliefs or accepting others' viewpoints. This can be a great strength when it stops us 'going along with' harmful ideas and behaviours. However, it's also important to show **empathy** to other people – to try to understand why they think and feel differently to us about what is right or fair, even if we don't agree with them at all.

Side quest

Find three (safe and non-breakable!) things in your house that are blue, then arrange them in an interesting way and take a picture of them. How creative can you get?

Working with your brain

It is no bad thing at all to feel deeply, to have a strong sense of right and wrong, and to push back against the injustices we see around us. In fact, I think the world would be a much better place if more people cared about making it as fair and kind as possible!

However, it is also important to keep a sense of balance. Although we might want to give everything of ourselves that we possibly can to stop an injustice, that isn't going to be **sustainable**. If we're not careful, our sensitivity – and the thoughts and actions that come with it – can leave us feeling **overwhelmed**, drained, defeated or even **burnt out**. We need to look after ourselves, not only because we deserve love and care, but also because the world needs us!

Justice sensitivity

Here are four ways to help with **justice sensitivity**:

1. Block out your distractions: One way to protect our **mental health** is to recognise that following world news can have a big impact on our justice-sensitive brains. Staying informed matters, but constant negative stories can make it harder to stay **resilient** and focus on meaningful action. It may be especially **traumatic** if you belong to a **marginalised** group and what you're reading feels personal.

That's why setting **boundaries** around the news you follow is really important. Setting and keeping boundaries isn't always easy for people with ADHD, but they are essential for protecting our own time, energy and **well-being**. Boundaries also help us support others, without neglecting ourselves.

Limiting the amount or kind of content you take in isn't selfish — it's self-preservation, like putting on your oxygen mask first on an aeroplane so you can help others better.

Here are some ways I set **boundaries** for myself – perhaps they can help you, too:

→ I stick to reading the news instead of watching videos, as I find that images and videos haunt and enrage me in an unhelpful way.

→ I avoid consuming news or upsetting information before bed.

→ I try to focus on longer, more in-depth articles or books rather than shock-value headlines and social media posts, and read bit by bit to avoid **overwhelming** myself.

→ I balance negative news stories by seeking out positive, hopeful ones.

→ I take breaks from consuming information online for a few days (or weeks!) if it's all feeling too much.

2. Talk to an adult: Standing up and **advocating** for yourself and others is important – but so is staying safe and looking after your mental **well-being**. If a situation feels overwhelming or upsetting, step away and speak to a trusted adult. They can help you process what's happening, come up with supportive ideas, and figure out how to take action in a way that protects you. Learning and making change is often easier – and more powerful – when you have someone to support you.

3. Find others who care: One important way to learn is by working together with others to make change and build community. Joining local youth campaigns and activism groups could help you meet others who care deeply about the same things as you. This can help you feel less alone and channel your strong feelings into positive, realistic action. Does your school have any groups you could join? If not, you could ask your trusted adult to help you search for ones near you, and check to see how they fit in with your schedule (see the Scaffolding section on page 249).

4. Keep calm: When we experience very strong feelings, we don't want to end up **impulsively** saying unhelpful, possibly hurtful things or doing anything else that we'll regret. We also don't want to put ourselves at unnecessary risk, or accidentally end up making a situation more heated and dangerous for the people we're trying to support.

Standing up for yourself

When it does feel safe to stand up for yourself or others, try to focus on staying as calm as possible. You can try out some of these ideas to see if they help:

→ Take deep breaths, especially before you speak. As well as calming your **nervous system**, it also gives you a bit of extra thinking time about what you want to say.

→ People should never call you names, make personal insults or threats, or physically touch you. You shouldn't do this to others either. If anyone is doing this, then it might be best to remove yourself until they calm down.

→ Our voices naturally get louder when we're angry or upset, so try to notice the volume of yours. Keeping your voice lower can help you feel more in control.

→ Try to properly listen to what people are saying and let them finish speaking before you respond (see pages 112–114). You can ask for the same from others.

→ If you feel yourself getting **overwhelmed** by emotions, take a break. This might mean walking away and finding a quiet spot to breathe and work through your feelings in peace, or even just turning away or lowering your head for a few seconds. 'Grounding techniques' – such as listing what you can see, hear and smell around you – can also help you feel calmer.

→ Focus on the action or idea that you disagree with, rather than the person doing or saying it. State any facts as simply and calmly as possible, and explain how you know the facts are true.

→ If you're giving your opinion or experience of something, and others may see things differently, recognise this by using words such as 'I feel ...' and 'It seems to me ...' rather than stating your view as a fact.

→ Where possible, try to think about finding solutions together rather than just proving you're right. Can you suggest a positive way forwards?

Side quest

What can you put in a bucket of water to make it weigh less?

Answer: A hole.

Rejection sensitivity

Just as with **justice sensitivity**, there are strategies to help you when you feel your **rejection sensitivity** kicking in. In the short term, here are three things you could try:

1. Talk it through: It can be really helpful to talk through your feelings with a trusted adult, who can give their outside view on the situation. You might decide that what seemed like a problem could have actually been a misunderstanding, or that what felt like a criticism may actually provide helpful feedback that you can learn something positive from.

2. Check in with others: If you still think that you have let someone down or disappointed them, remember that rejection sensitivity can make it likely you're thinking that things are worse than they are! Rather than assuming what someone feels and creating a bigger issue (perhaps where there wasn't one at all), try calmly talking to the person to try to better understand.

3. Write it down: It might be easier to write a message, so you can choose your words carefully and take a break if things feel tricky. If you feel comfortable, you could explain about your rejection sensitivity and talk about ways to communicate in future that make it easier on you.

Here are some ideas to help you deal with **rejection sensitivity** in the longer term:

1. Practise while you're calm: When you're feeling rejected and experiencing strong emotions, it can be pretty hard to calm yourself down. Try practising some self-soothing strategies, such as deep breathing or squeezing a squishy ball, with a trusted adult when you are feeling calm. Write down what works in a notebook to help you remember. Then, you can try putting them into action when something **triggers** you.

2. Accept imperfection: It's not possible to avoid all negative feedback, disagreements or 'failures' – and it wouldn't be a good thing if we could! We can learn a lot from these experiences, and this can help us grow as people. The reality is that nobody's perfect, and that means you aren't either! Sometimes you're going to make mistakes, and do things that annoy or upset people, because that's true for every human.

3. Build resilience: Although it can feel so hard when we experience rejection sensitivity, every time we go through it, we are building up proof for our brain that we can handle it – and that things are usually nowhere near as bad as we've imagined. This can help develop our **resilience**.

GOOD JOB!

You can learn more about resilience on page 200.

139

4. Embrace differences: **Rejection sensitivity** has been linked to low **self-esteem**, which research suggests people with ADHD experience more often than **neurotypical** people. Given that we often think and behave in different ways to neurotypical people, it is understandable that we might end up feeling down on ourselves. But there is nothing 'wrong' or 'weird' about you, so don't be afraid to ignore or challenge (if it feels safe to do so) those who suggest otherwise.

5. Shift your focus: It has been suggested that people with rejection sensitivity might find it trickier to focus on tasks, because so much of their mental energy is being put into detecting and avoiding possible sources of rejection. To help take our brains off this 'high-alert' rejection-sensitive mode, where they're over-working to protect us from being hurt, we can build our self-esteem so that we value and believe in ourselves. There are some ideas on pages 241–248 to help you do this.

Which of these elephant claims to fame is true?

A) They are the largest living land animals.

B) They can communicate through vibrations in the ground, which they sense with their feet.

C) They can use their trunk like a snorkel to breathe while underwater.

D) They have the best sense of smell of any known animal.

E) All of the above.

Answer: E) All of the above.

Brain break
Facts, games and ADHD-friendly activities to give your brain a rest

Experts think that an elephant's trunk may be the most sensitive body part of any animal in the world! There are around 400,000 **neurons** in the bundle of nerves that controls an elephant's trunk, which is a lot more than scientists expected.

Elephants use their trunk, which is a combined nose and upper lip, for everything from grabbing, smelling, breathing and calling others, to comforting babies and sucking up water to drink (by squirting it into their mouths) or to give themselves a shower!

Why is ADHD only a thing in rich countries?

It isn't! But ADHD is often misunderstood in this way – and particularly thought of as 'an American thing', likely because the USA has had such a leading role in ADHD research.

In recent years, some wealthier countries have seen more widespread awareness of ADHD, which may have helped more families and professionals to recognise ADHD **traits**. However, multiple studies have found significant (often similar) rates of ADHD in lower-income and middle-income countries around the world.

Side quest

Try using crumpled paper to make art that looks like an elephant's tough, wrinkled skin! Scrunch up a piece of paper and use paint or felt-tip pens to cover it with colour. Then open it out to reveal your creation!

Scientists have discovered that elephants have one of the largest and most complex brains of any land animal. An adult elephant's brain weighs about 5 kilograms and contains an astonishing 257 billion **neurons**, far more than in the human brain!

Elephants use their enormous brains to build deep and lasting relationships. They seem to recognise and remember other elephants after years apart. A 2024 study even suggested that elephants remember the scent of humans who they haven't seen for as long as 13 years!

Chapter eight
Chameleon

Chameleon

Paying attention to everything at once

Struggle

It's pretty hard to get anything past a chameleon! Their amazing eyes can move in completely different directions at the same time, swivelling around to give them almost perfect 360-degree vision. Sometimes, having an ADHD-wired brain can feel a bit like looking at the world through a chameleon's all-seeing eyes — but not always in helpful ways.

Neurotypical brains usually focus on a few particular things around them that seem the most important, and filter out the rest so it fades into the background. However, with ADHD, the brain often notices everything all at once without automatically **prioritising** in the same way.

When someone is talking, our attention might be grabbed by, say, the buzz of a bee flying across the room — but it's not because we're bored or being bad listeners! It's just that our busy brains don't 'turn the volume down' on everything else. It all carries on competing for our attention, and our brains don't know what to focus on.

This super-sensitivity to our surroundings isn't just distracting when we want to focus on something – it can also be **overwhelming**. The constant flood of sights, sounds, smells and other sensations can easily leave us feeling **overstimulated**, especially in noisy, crowded places. This can make us feel tired, anxious, confused, irritated and even panicky.

Side quest

Can you find the hidden chameleon?

Strength

A chameleon's all-seeing eyes give it a serious advantage in the animal kingdom. As it takes in its surroundings, a chameleon can see things that another animal might well miss – whether that's a tasty-looking grasshopper resting on a branch above its head, or a deadly tree snake silently slithering up behind it.

In a similar (but not life-and-death!) way, distractable ADHD brains may end up noticing things that others don't. Even when you're trying to focus on one particular thing, your mind may still be open to everything else – and this openness can also help you come up with wildly creative ideas that others might find it harder to reach.

Studies have shown that people with ADHD tend to show higher levels of 'divergent thinking' – that is, coming up with lots of new, original ideas for a single problem.

One way that scientists measure divergent thinking is through the Alternative Uses Test, where people are asked to think of as many uses as possible for a simple object such as a shoe, a brick or a paper clip. Let's give it a quick go, just for fun!

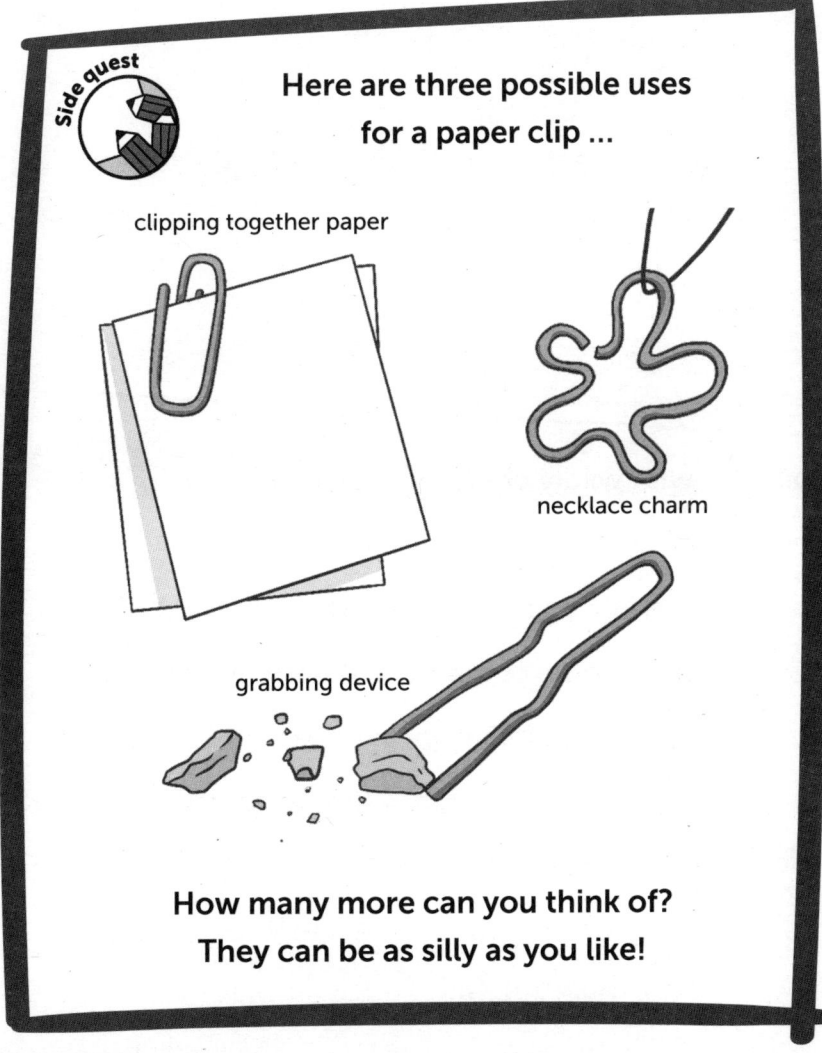

Side quest

Here are three possible uses for a paper clip ...

clipping together paper

necklace charm

grabbing device

How many more can you think of?
They can be as silly as you like!

Working with your brain

When you're finding it hard to focus because there are so many distractions around you, the first thing to remember is that ADHD makes this genuinely more difficult for you. Give yourself a break!

Brain science

Studies have shown that people with ADHD may have exceptionally active connections between the parts of the brain that help it decide what's important to pay attention to. It's these active connections that may cause **ADHDers** to notice 'irrelevant' things in our field of vision.

You may feel like you need to **mask**, especially if you're with another person or a group of people, and pretend that you're not noticing (or being distracted by) the sights, sounds and other things that keep catching your attention. This is understandable, but it can put even more pressure on you, making you feel even more frustrated and **overwhelmed**.

You can read more about masking on page 110.

These strategies could help you find your focus:

Be honest

It's fine just to tell people that your ADHD means that staying focused isn't always easy. People can sometimes misread each other, so being honest and open can avoid any misunderstandings — like them thinking you're just bored or not listening. However, if you're trying your best and you've explained why you're distracted, but they won't listen or don't believe you, then that's really their problem — not yours!

Embrace the fidget

Some ADHDers find that allowing themselves to **stim** — playing with a fidget toy, doodling, chewing gum, squeezing a stress ball, tapping your foot, and so on — can help them focus, too.

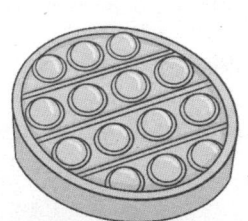
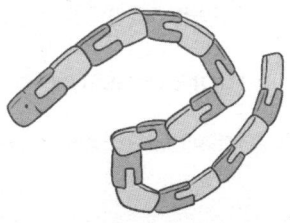

Block out your distractions

When you really want to focus, physically blocking out distractions can be helpful:

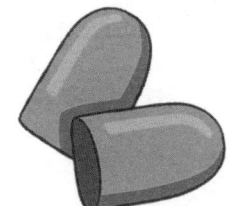

➡️ Earplugs can help to silence or muffle sounds. If you still need to be able to hear certain things, like a teacher's instructions or a friend talking to you, there are earplugs that just reduce sound a bit.

➡️ You could also try wearing headphones, with or without music playing. A lot of people with ADHD find music with no words helps them focus. Try searching for the terms 'binaural beats' or 'lo-fi beats', or for playlists with names like 'study music'.

➡️ If you sit facing towards a wall or a corner of a room, there'll be fewer distractions to catch your eye. Try sitting away from a window if there are distractions outside. It could be helpful to wear a hoodie with the hood up or even thick-rimmed glasses or sunglasses if you get distracted by what's going on to your sides.

What works for one **ADHDer** won't work for another, so try building your own checklist of what helps you block out when you want to focus. Keep it handy, perhaps in a pocket notebook.

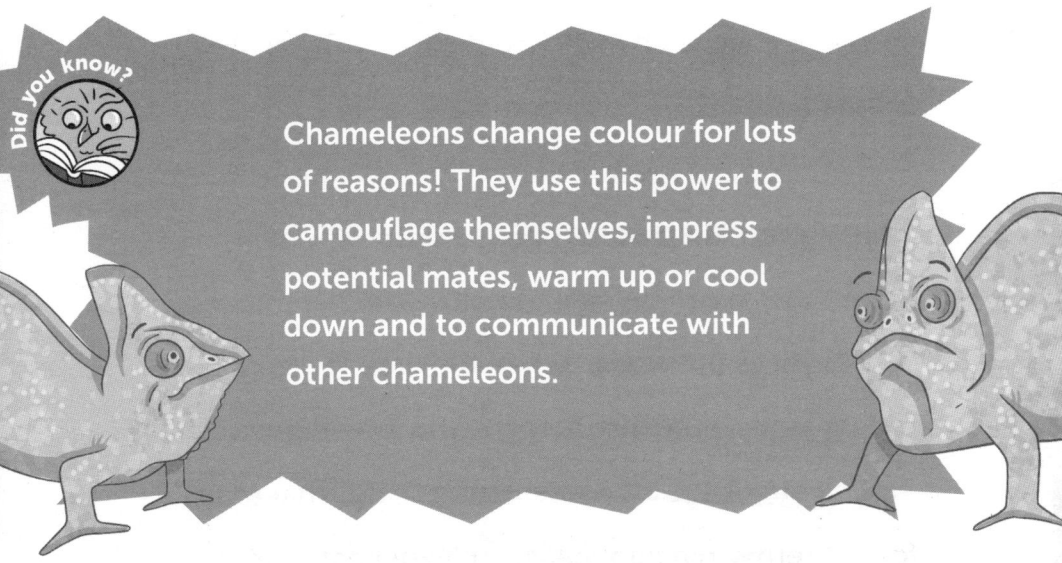

Chameleons change colour for lots of reasons! They use this power to camouflage themselves, impress potential mates, warm up or cool down and to communicate with other chameleons.

Find your flow

Anti-distraction aids and strategies can sometimes help you get into a **flow state**, where you're lost in what you're doing. You may well find that you then naturally stop tuning in to distractions so much. If you enter **hyperfocus** (see the Cheetah chapter on page 179), you may actually be much less distractable in that state than a **neurotypical** person usually is!

Ask for adjustments

Depending on what country you live in, your school and future workplace may be required by law to allow reasonable adjustments for your ADHD. This could include allowing you to use headphones or a fidget spinner, move to sit in different spots or have more breaks and extra time to complete tasks.

Enjoy your distractions!

Sometimes it can be nice to enjoy your heightened sensitivity to the world. When the time feels right, try letting yourself be distracted – and drawing or writing about the little interesting things that grab your attention. Who knows what your amazing brain will create?

Brain break
Facts, games and ADHD-friendly
activities to give your brain a rest

There's a chameleon that, as a fully grown adult, is about the size of a pumpkin seed! It's called the nano-chameleon, or *Brookesia nana*, and it lives in the rainforest in Madagascar. Its tiny, swivelling eyes look all the way around it as it searches for prey — particularly mites so small that humans can't see them without a microscope!

Try drawing *Brookesia nana* at its actual size! You could trace this pumpkin seed to use as a size guide.

IRRITATING ADHD QUESTIONS:

Isn't everyone 'a little bit ADHD'?

No, it doesn't work like that! Everyone gets distracted sometimes, and forgets things occasionally, but that's very different from it happening so many times a day that you often end up feeling exhausted, frustrated and **overwhelmed**.

Think about it like this: everyone has trouble getting to sleep sometimes, but that's very different from someone with insomnia lying awake for hours at night and then having to fight to get through every day.

To be **diagnosed** with ADHD, your symptoms have to negatively affect you and be constant enough to have a big impact on your life.

There seems to be a link between some forms of **neurodivergence** and being super flexible (having 'hypermobility') around your joints. In a 2022 study, around 50 per cent of the participants who were **autistic** or had ADHD or **Tourette syndrome** were also hypermobile, compared to just 20 per cent of **neurotypical** people.

Scientists aren't sure why this might be, but it's a big enough difference to be worth looking into! They're also exploring other possible links between neurodivergence and various physical conditions.

Do you think you're hypermobile? I am — I have to be careful not to overbend when doing yoga!

A chameleon's tongue is typically around twice the length of its body. Most of the time, it sits neatly folded up inside the chameleon's mouth. But when it's time to catch some prey for dinner, that tongue shoots out at incredible speed — in fact, the tongues of some tiny chameleon species are even faster than top sports cars!

At the very end of a chameleon's tongue is a soft, muscular little bulb that works like a suction cup, covered in super-sticky mucus. This specialised tongue tip is so effective that it can grab prey weighing up to a third of the chameleon's body weight!

**Side quest**

Copy these three lines. Can you turn them into something else entirely?

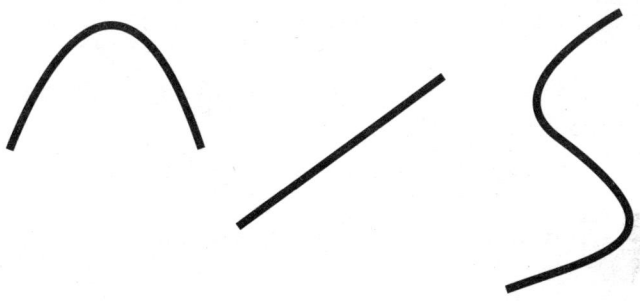

How about a dog, a face or a ship at sea? What else can you come up with?

Chapter nine
Loris

Loris
Zoning out and daydreaming

Struggle

With its slow, gentle movements and huge, glassy eyes, the dreamy-looking loris is one of nature's most adorable animals. But if you're an **ADHDer** who often gets lost in your own thoughts, you might not find your own daydreamy tendencies quite so charming!

ADHDers, particularly those of us with **inattentive** or **combined type ADHD**, are as likely to get distracted by our own thoughts as by things going on around us. We may not even notice this is happening until someone or something interrupts our mind's wanderings – and then we'll suddenly realise that we have no idea what has been going on outside of our own heads. Although our bodies are still where we left them, it's like our brains have been somewhere else entirely.

Sometimes, our mind's dreamy and distracted journeying can be quite enjoyable. We might be thinking about big questions or interesting things we've seen, or reliving and imagining fun moments. At other times, it can lead us through an endless maze of anxious, obsessive or negative thoughts that leave us totally drained. Either way, when we snap back to reality, we may not always get the friendliest welcome.

See, other people don't know what's going on in our heads. If we start to daydream in the middle of a conversation with someone, they might think that we don't really care about what they're saying (especially if they don't know much about ADHD). But this isn't the case at all — our brains just slip away more easily into our own thoughts.

Even if no one noticed us zoning out — or did, but understood why and didn't take it personally — there's still the worrying possibility that we missed something important. This could be anything from a teacher telling us an exam date to a friend trying to share something meaningful. We may also space out while travelling somewhere, so we end up going the wrong way and being late. We may not even know what we missed, which can cause us anxiety and confusion.

Strength

Your brain is powerful, mysterious and entirely unique to you. When your mind wanders, it may be missing what's going on around you – and that's often far from ideal. However, it's also giving you a fascinating insight into your own thoughts, ideas and imagination.

Brain science

Certain parts of our brain are responsible for our ability to reflect on our own thoughts and engage with imagination and ideas, rather than just the material world around us. Together, these brain areas form the so-called **default mode network (DMN).** Scientists have found that the DMN is especially active in people with ADHD, which means that our attention is pulled away towards unrelated thoughts and we daydream more often.

Spending time with our thoughts and daydreams can be fun and relaxing, and can help us get to know ourselves better. We can build a rich inner life where we're free to play, create and explore. This may help us handle times when the outside world feels particularly tough, boring or ADHD-unfriendly.

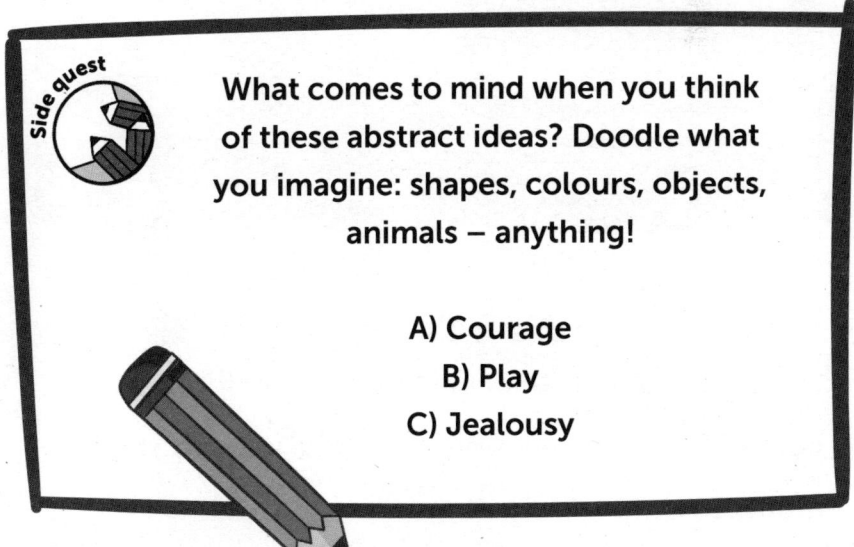

Experts also think types of daydreaming that include playful images, creative thinking and positive wishes can actually be **productive** as well as enjoyable. We can use this kind of daydreaming as a 'practice zone' for thinking through ideas and plans that we want to develop, and for rehearsing future situations.

Side quest

What comes to mind when you think of these abstract ideas? Doodle what you imagine: shapes, colours, objects, animals — anything!

A) Courage
B) Play
C) Jealousy

Working with your brain

Not being able to stay present and focused on a task, and not being able to listen when spoken to directly because your mind is elsewhere, are some of the most common and noticeable **traits** linked to ADHD. Experts use these more than any others to make their **diagnoses**. Try not to be too hard on yourself if and when you do space out – it's part of a recognised condition, not a sign that you don't care!

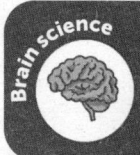

Brain science

Research has shown that, if we have ADHD, the **DMN** often doesn't switch off even if we need to focus on a task, such as doing homework or tidying up. This makes it easier for our brain to slip back into 'daydreaming mode' instead of focusing on the task.

Looking more closely at what might be causing your zoning-out, rather than judging yourself for doing it, could help you develop some helpful ways to stay more present:

Spot the situations

Are there certain situations in which you tend to daydream a lot? Perhaps it's in class when someone is reading aloud or doing a presentation, or when you have to write a long piece of work? If you can't think of any, try to notice when you catch yourself zoning out over the next few days. Note down those moments and try to find any patterns.

Some experts believe that children and young people may daydream in class because they're finding the work too easy. Is this true for you? Perhaps your brain is trying to give you something more interesting and exciting to think about while you wait for others to finish their work?

Face your fears

'Spacing out' can also be a coping mechanism, a way for your brain to handle something that it finds uncomfortable or difficult. This could be when you're feeling bored, **overwhelmed** or afraid — for instance, if school work feels too hard or you're not sure how to manage a tricky situation.

A trusted adult might help things feel more manageable if you think your brain is trying to close itself off from things that are too challenging or high-pressured. This might mean extra one-to-one support in a tricky subject, or a daily **brain dump** about any worries you may have.

Take a break

Is your brain exhausted, perhaps from the effort of **masking** and trying to meet the demands of everyday life? You may need a break in the short term, to lighten your mental load and to build in more regular rest time. Check in with your basic physical needs, too — people with ADHD often don't get enough sleep, drink enough water or have regular meals, which can make focusing even harder!

There's more about accidentally neglecting our needs in the Bee chapter on page 51.

Super stimming!

Are things moving at too slow a pace for you? You could try leaning in to something that you may already be doing naturally ... fidgeting! This is also known as **stimming** (self-stimulatory behaviour).

Brain science

Recent research suggests that physical movement, such as fidgeting with your hands, can help boost the brain's focus and attention. It does this by increasing levels of certain chemicals (**dopamine** and **noradrenaline**) in the brain.

Here are some low-key stimming actions that could help when you're in class or somewhere else that's quiet:

Rubbing your fingers and thumbs together

Doodling, scribbling or taking notes

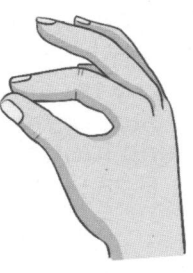

→ Touching your fingertips together in turn

→ Gently squeezing and releasing your muscles

→ 'Cricket legs': rubbing your foot against your lower leg

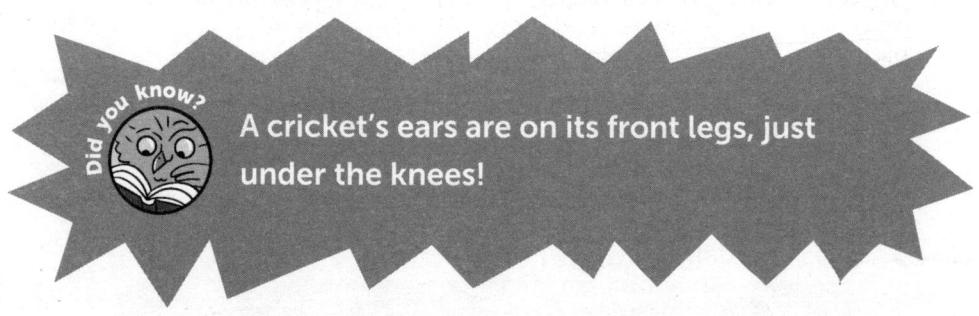

Did you know?

A cricket's ears are on its front legs, just under the knees!

You and a trusted adult could speak to others and help them to understand about **stimming** and how it helps you to focus, so that you don't need to worry about feeling self-conscious or someone asking you to stop. Depending on where you live, stopping you from stimming may actually be against the law.

In some countries (for example in the UK, where ADHD is a recognised disability), you may also be able to get funding to help you pay for stimming tools such as fidget toys and rocking footrests.

Engaged listening

When someone is talking directly to you, engaged listening techniques can help you stay focused and prevent your brain wandering off into daydream land. You could try to:

- React physically (nodding or shaking your head, for example)
- React verbally (saying 'mmm', 'oh!', 'uh-huh' and so on)
- Ask questions
- Summarise in your mind what they're saying

If you feel comfortable, just be honest when you do zone out. Ask the speaker to repeat what they've said, and explain that it's not personal – just ADHD!

Brain science

People with ADHD are more likely to experience negative or obsessive thoughts while daydreaming. This may be linked to **maladaptive daydreaming** or a condition called **obsessive-compulsive disorder (OCD)**. Make sure you talk to a trusted adult if you experience any difficult, draining thoughts and daydreams.

 **Side quest**

Draw a big, looping scribble. Then colour in all the completed loops!

Meditation

Meditation is a kind of peaceful exercise for the mind, where people aim to clear their thoughts for a while and enjoy a sense of quiet calm. Some people think that regularly meditating – even for just a couple of minutes each day – can also help get your brain more used to being directed in certain ways. Over time, it could help you stay focused on the present and redirect negative thoughts towards more positive ones. Ask a trusted adult to help you look up some ADHD-friendly meditations that you could try, including walking meditations and guided breathing.

Enjoy getting lost!

If you enjoy getting lost in your thoughts and daydreams, when the time feels right try just letting your mind wander! You never know what your brilliant brain could come up with.

Brain break

Facts, games and ADHD-friendly activities to give your brain a rest

Don't be fooled by a slow loris's cute, fuzzy, dreamy-eyed little face — it can be deadly, even to humans! It oozes venom (that stinks of sweaty socks!) from glands on the insides of its upper arms. It licks these glands to transfer the venom to its mouth, and then bites down with its sharp, strong teeth.

When slow loris mums leave their babies to look for food, they lick these glands and then groom the babies' fur so they're covered in venom. This is thought to put off predators, such as sun bears and clouded leopards.

Have you tried avoiding sugar? That's what causes ADHD, right?

Not right! Many researchers have looked into the relationship between ADHD and sugar. Some have found that when some **hyperactive** children eat a lot of sugar, they become more restless. Others have found that some children are more easily distracted when they have high-sugar diets. However, most have found no such link – and, in any case, this is a long way from sugar 'causing' ADHD.

We still don't know exactly what causes ADHD, but it seems to run in families. Scientists think that **genetics** is likely a major factor.

Draw a very short comic strip turning the super-powered, venomous slow loris into a superhero — or a supervillain!

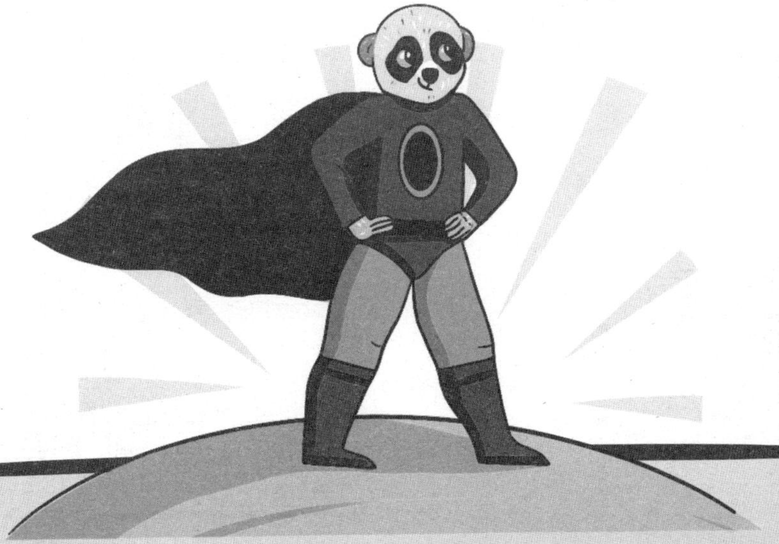

 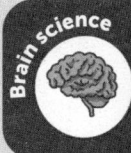
A 2018 study found that almost 1 in 3 business-owners are **ADHDers**, even though only around 1 in 20 adults has ADHD!

All lorises have two tongues. They use the top one for drinking nectar, and the bottom one for cleaning their teeth!

Chapter ten
Cheetah

Cheetah

Focusing in intense bursts

Strength

The cheetah is the world's fastest land animal, running at up to 120 kilometres per hour! When it's going at full speed, no other animal can touch it. This makes it one of the most successful hunters in its environment.

Many (but not all) people with ADHD can enter a similar 'turbo-boost' mode, known as **hyperfocus**. This is a state of intense concentration, typically on something that interests us, that can last for hours and hours on end. During hyperfocus, we don't really notice time passing, and everything other than the task in hand seems to fade away entirely.

Not only is this very different to how **ADHDers** stay focused, it can actually go far beyond the average **neurotypical** person's level of concentration. Some people with ADHD (including me!) can hyperfocus so intensely that we sometimes don't notice people literally shouting our name or waving their hands in front of us.

When ADHDers hyperfocus, we may be able to get a huge amount done in a relatively short time – sometimes an amount that seems almost impossible. This can be extremely helpful, especially if we have left things until the last moment! It can also give us an edge when getting started with a project, as we may keep learning and practising long after neurotypical people have had enough.

Hyperfocus can be satisfying, enjoyable and even relaxing, as we can lose ourselves in a particular subject and leave behind other worries and demands. People can hyperfocus on anything from video games and knitting to researching the possibility of life on Mars, and have a lot of fun doing it!

Struggle

As useful as **hyperfocus** can be for **ADHDers**, it can also take its toll on our bodies and minds. When we're deep in hyperfocus, we may not notice that we haven't eaten, had a drink, moved, slept or even been to the toilet. Or we may be aware of these needs but not want, or feel able, to break our focus to look after ourselves.

This is one of the reasons why thinking of hyperfocus as a positive 'superpower' can be unhelpful. It can make you feel that your productivity – how much you can do – is more important than your **well-being**. In case it needs saying: this is never true!

ADHDers may be tempted to rely on hyperfocus to get things done, but It's a risky strategy because we often can't control what we hyperfocus on. You could find that your brain locks on to something else and you spend hours and hours doing something completely different from what you'd planned.

This might be something fun, and even useful, but it isn't ideal when you have other urgent tasks to do. For example, you might hyperfocus on a new video game instead of getting homework done for the next day. After a period of hyperfocus, you may no longer have the energy to get the top-priority things done at all. This could ultimately cause you more stress.

Side quest

Different people can (and can't) wiggle different parts of their face. Stand in front of a mirror and try to wiggle your eyebrows, ears and nose.

Can you wiggle them up and down, side to side or not at all?

Working with your brain

After a sprint, a cheetah needs to lie down and rest for an hour or more until they've recovered. This is something worth keeping in mind when it comes to **hyperfocus**. Such an intense state of concentration takes a lot out of us, and too much of it – especially if it isn't being balanced with proper rest – can lead to mental and physical exhaustion.

Brain science

Hyperfocus seems to be related to an imbalance of **dopamine** and **noradrenaline** – chemicals in the brain that help with focus and **motivation**. When something feels really fun or interesting, the brain can zoom in and focus super hard on it.

Strangely, this is also what makes it hard to pay attention! It can be tricky for us to 'switch gears' – both to stop doing things that we find enjoyable and to start tasks that we find less interesting.

Give yourself a break

Pulling yourself out of hyperfocus might not be easy because you may *want* to keep pushing through necessary tasks – perhaps to make up for time when you were distracted. You may feel like you don't have time to rest, or that you'll risk 'falling behind' if you do.

However, if the expectations on you require this kind of exhausting effort, maybe *they* need to change – or perhaps you need a lot more support to fulfil them in a healthy, **sustainable** way. You and your wonderfully wild brain need and deserve rest.

Managing hyperfocus

Try these four strategies to help you manage your **hyperfocus**:

1. Set out supplies and stop-watches: When you start an activity or project that you enjoy or feel **motivated** to complete, place plenty of water and enough snacks nearby. Set two alarms: one for the time when you want to finish and one for five minutes before (to let you know when your time is nearly up).

If possible, ask someone to come and check on you when they hear the second alarm. Just remember that you may feel grumpy or stressed if someone interrupts your hyperfocus, even if you've asked them to!

2. Make possible plans: It can be helpful to look ahead at what you want to do today and tomorrow, and make some plans so that you have a good reason to stop when the time comes. Hyperfocus can be joyful – but it can also go on too long and cause you stress, or make you miss out on other things. That means this feel-good moment can lead to disappointment later.

If you do have some flexibility though, there's nothing wrong with surfing the wave of your hyperfocus. You could even set aside dedicated time for hyperfocus, to lose yourself in a favourite activity.

Brain science

Hyperfocus is associated with other forms of **neurodivergence** too, including **autism**. However, ADHD hyperfocus seems to be generally more unpredictable in nature, with **ADHDers** often getting wrapped up in whatever happens to catch our attention, rather than what we might need to do or a particular interest.

3. Learn from your hyperfocus: Think about what tends to lead to **hyperfocus**, and see if you can recreate some of those focus-friendly conditions. These could help get you into a helpful (but less intense) **flow state** when you're feeling distracted. It might not always work, but it may be worth a try if something as simple as headphones or a particular spot on the sofa seems to settle your mind a bit.

4. Take it easy: There's a lot of information and different ideas to take in, I know! **ADHDers** often overload ourselves trying to do everything at once. Start off by trying just one of the ideas above – or something else you think might help.

What will you pick first? Remember, you can always try something else later!

Brain break
Facts, games and ADHD-friendly activities to give your brain a rest

Mum of the Year award for cheetahs! A female cheetah gives birth to 2–8 cubs at a time, and raises them all on her own. She hides her cubs in a den in the long grass or bushes while she hunts, to keep them out of sight of predators.

If a cheetah mum suspects that a predator may be nearby, she moves her family to a new place to keep them safe. The cubs stay with their mum until they are up to two years old, and are able to take care of themselves.

 Side quest

Trace this cheetah and cover it in spots! Every cheetah has its own unique pattern of spots, a bit like human fingerprints.

 Did you know?

The dark markings on a cheetah's face, which run from its eyes down to the sides of its mouth, are often known as 'tear lines'. Scientists think they stop too much bright sunlight getting in a cheetah's eyes, so that it can see its prey better while it's hunting.

In some sports, such as American football, players often wear black make-up under their eyes for the same reason — even though they're chasing a ball, not an antelope!

Brain science

Do certain sounds — like chewing, tapping, coughing, scratching or even loud breathing — annoy or stress you out so much that you feel like you could explode? You might be experiencing 'sound rage', which is also called misophonia. It has been associated with ADHD, **autism** and **OCD**.

Many people find some human-made sounds annoying or gross, but misophonia makes these feelings so extreme that the sound becomes unbearable. People with misophonia often try putting on music or distracting themselves with a task to avoid the noise and calm down.

It's only boys that get ADHD, right?

People of any gender can have ADHD. Boys are still around three times more likely to be diagnosed with ADHD than girls, but this could be partly due to social factors – such as expectations for girls to behave in certain ways – rather than because it's actually more common in boys. For many girls, ADHD traits, such as hyperactivity, occur inside their minds rather than on the outside, so it's not as easy for others to spot their differences.

Most ADHD-related research and resources have tended to focus on white boys and men, so symptoms in other genders and ethnic identities may be missed or misunderstood. People from marginalised groups, such as Black women and girls, are less likely to get proper diagnosis and support. Although this has started changing in recent years, we've still got a lot further to go.

Which of these words is the odd one out?

pride

pencil

crash

herd

waddle

Answer: Pencil – because all the others are collective nouns for groups of animals.

Did you know?

A cheetah typically has between 2,000 and 3,000 spots!

Chapter eleven
Blue whale

Blue whale

Getting stuck between tasks

Struggle

The blue whale is the largest animal ever known to have lived on Earth. It's as long as three buses, and its tongue alone weighs as much as an elephant! This huge, awe-inspiring creature glides through the ocean with grace and ease, cruising through the blue waters of its marine home.

However, quickly stopping, starting or changing direction isn't easy for this gentle giant. If a blue whale gets into difficulty or loses its way, it can end up getting stuck in shallow water or on land, not being able to move.

ADHDers can sometimes feel similarly stuck when we're trying to start or finish a task, or switch between different tasks that we need to do. This is because we tend to experience challenges with **executive functions**, which are the mental abilities that help make all these things happen.

Executive functions are complex mental processes and abilities that are involved in planning, decision-making, organisation, focusing attention and more. Together, they help us to regulate (control) and adapt our thoughts, feelings and actions in our day-to-day lives. They're linked to the front part of the brain, specifically the prefrontal cortex.

Studies have shown that some parts of the prefrontal cortex are less active in people with ADHD. This may explain why our executive functions often work differently.

People with ADHD often experience a 'gap' between the strong desire to do a task and the ability to follow through with it. Most people without ADHD do not experience this – and, if they do, their executive functions may make it easier to push through. This can lead to our experience being misunderstood and minimised, especially by those who are doing the same task and just cannot appreciate why it might be different for us.

It can be incredibly frustrating to feel stuck in this gap, not through laziness or lack of interest, but because our brain's processes don't help us out in the same way. It can take a lot longer to make progress, which may make us just want to abandon our task altogether.

Difficulties with task-switching may seem particularly unfair (they do to me, anyway) because an **ADHDer's** brain is often happy to jump into all sorts of shiny, new tasks and projects – just apparently not the ones we want it to focus on!

Strength

The positive side of having to put in so much effort to start, finish and change tasks might not be immediately obvious – but trust me, it exists!

Although ADHDers' **executive function** challenges may make it feel like we're having to live life on 'hard mode', working to support ourselves through them can help us to develop an incredibly helpful mindset that will become a great strength for us.

Many studies have shown that we can improve our executive functions through practice. So, when things feel impossibly hard, we can find an opportunity to develop our **growth mindset** (see page 241): an attitude of positive thinking about what we can achieve. It can help us to remember that the efforts we're making now will benefit us in future.

Developing a **growth mindset**, in turn, helps to build our **resilience**: an inner strength that can really help us handle life's challenges. We can better trust in our ability to do hard things, and work through the tricky feelings that may come up while doing them, because we have proof that we've already done this in the past and we know we can do it again. These are essential, lifelong skills that can be applied across all sorts of situations.

Starting, completing and switching tasks can also give us good opportunities to practise our self-compassion (see page 244) and self-acceptance. Our struggles with these important everyday things are real, unfair and not our fault, and we deserve acknowledgement and **compassion** for this – from ourselves as much as anyone else!

As well as making our minds much nicer places to be, this can help us in a practical way. When we accept the reality of our differences, we can support ourselves in useful, ADHD-friendly ways and work at learning strategies to help us. Rather than just scolding and shaming ourselves for not meeting society's expectations, we may actually improve our ability to get things done. Experts have linked negative self-talk to poorer performance and learning, and positive self-talk to better results. So let's learn to be kind to ourselves!

I DID MY BEST.

I'M PROUD OF MYSELF.

I AM RESILIENT AND CAN OVERCOME CHALLENGES.

See pages 241–248 for tips on developing your growth mindset and self-compassion.

Working with your brain

Like a blue whale, your brain is a powerful and majestic force of nature that just needs a bit more time, space and support to avoid getting (and staying) stuck!

It's important to remember that finding it hard to get started on a task isn't the same as being lazy. 'Lazy' isn't a super-helpful word at the best of times, but it is usually defined as 'not wanting to work or make any effort'.

A 'lazy afternoon' typically describes an enjoyably relaxed time that requires no, or very little, effort. Does this sound like it describes someone with ADHD trying over and over again to start, change or finish a task, getting more and more frustrated and upset? To me, that's the exact opposite!

What we're experiencing is a genuine biological difference, as real as a short-sighted student struggling to read what the teacher has written on the board in class. Would you say that they're just not trying hard enough? Does the fact that other children in the class can see OK mean that they're making it up?

Of course not! They just have different needs, and only accepting and meeting these needs — for instance, with aids such as glasses — will actually help. The same goes for ADHD.

 Side quest

What links these four words?

STRAW

BLACK

BLUE

RASP

Answer: They are all types of berries!

These tips might help you to get your brain moving:

Step by step

When you're finding it really tricky to get started on a task, try breaking it down into smaller steps that you can tackle one by one. Even if a task feels like it should be so 'easy' that breaking it down seems silly, try to remember that there is no such thing as a universally easy or difficult task. If it's hard for you, that's all that matters.

For example, let's say you need to put your clothes away. What's the tiniest step possible? Could you open your wardrobe door? Could you put away one sock? You might want to write each step down, with an empty tick box next to it, and then tick it off when you're done.

Ticking off a task can give us a nice, confidence-boosting sense of achievement, and a little **dopamine** boost that can help us carry on and do more. Just focus on that very first step to get yourself going!

If you're working on a new, unfamiliar task or starting a larger, complicated project, try asking a trusted adult to help you plan exactly what you need to do. They can help you break down the work into smaller steps, and set progress goals to keep you on track. Clearly understanding what you need to do can boost your confidence, and help you stop procrastinating – putting off the task by doing something else – because you're feeling **overwhelmed** or are worried about getting it wrong.

PUT SOCK AWAY ✓

PUT SHIRT AWAY

Ready, set, go!

Timed bursts can also be very helpful in breaking down a task so it feels more manageable. They can create a sense of against-the-clock urgency that can fire up some people with ADHD.

For instance, if you're finding it really tricky to get started on your maths homework, try setting a timer for five minutes and seeing how much you can get done in that time. Then maybe try another five minutes, and see how much more you can do. Competition can be a helpful **motivator** – so try competing against yourself!

Take a break

Sometimes, our brains might be feeling a bit too **overwhelmed** to jump into something new right away. Do you ever get a stuck, spinning-on-the-spot feeling when you try to move from one task to the next right away, or to get started on a task the moment you arrive somewhere? I know I do! It's almost like my brain hasn't caught up with the change, and it needs a little breather to realise that we're going to do something new.

Try giving yourself a bit of a break between tasks and events: a couple of minutes or more to let your brain rest before you make any more demands of it.

During this time, you could listen to a song, count your breaths, stare off into space and daydream ... whatever you need.

Try to avoid watching short videos or playing around on a tablet or smartphone. This can feel relaxing, but isn't actually very restful: it's still asking your brain to take in more information.

Sometimes, it isn't easy to stop and shift our attention on to a new task because we're in a state of hyperfocus. You can learn more about hyperfocus in the Cheetah chapter on page 179.

Mix it up!

We're animals, not machines, so our brains respond differently to the same strategies on different days!

Try out some different ideas – you can start with one from this section. If you find one that works for you, stick with it – until it stops working so well. You can then give another strategy a go, and maybe use different ones each week, depending on how you feel.

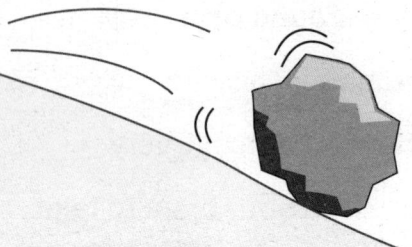

Be a rolling stone!

A common piece of advice for getting things done is to 'eat the frog', which means doing the hardest task first so it's out of the way. The idea is that the boost of confidence from completing this tricky task will also make the rest of your tasks seem a lot easier. It works for many people (and might do for you!) but lots of **ADHDers** (including me) find that this 'hardest thing first' approach makes us freeze up so that we don't get anything done. What works better for me, and apparently many others with ADHD, is the exact opposite – let's call it the 'rolling stone' method.

→ List out the tasks that you need to get done, breaking them down into smaller steps if it helps. Try not to overload yourself with too many tasks – three to five is often a good number.

→ Choose a task that feels like the easiest or quickest one, and get started on it. (Sometimes I leave the last sentence or two of what I'm writing to finish the next morning. This then becomes the 'quick win' task that gets me started!)

→ When you've completed your first task, tick it off and celebrate! Then try to tick off one or two tasks that feel a bit harder.

In this way, work your way up to the hardest task (with breaks along the way). By this time, you'll hopefully have built up some confidence and **momentum**, so it's easier to get into working in a helpful **flow state**.

I think of this as the 'rolling stone' method because we just give ourselves a small nudge (an easier task) to get started, then pick up speed and power as we go, which helps us tackle the harder tasks later on. The only thing to be careful of is not trying to fit too much in, so we have enough time and mental energy left for the hardest task – especially if it's urgent. Ask a trusted adult to help you try this for the first time.

Body doubling

Body doubling means working on a task with at least one other person present, either in the room or virtually. They don't have to even help you with the task – they just have to quietly be there. It may sound simple, but for many people it works brilliantly! It seems to be particularly popular among **neurodivergent** communities, including people with ADHD. There are a few different ideas as to

why body doubling works, from making us feel like part of a team to reminding us to stay on task, but no one knows for sure. If you're finding it tricky to start a task, or to stick with it, you could ask a family member or friend to try a body doubling session.

Set a timer for a certain length of time, such as 30 minutes or an hour.

Before you start the timer, tell each other what you're planning to get done in this time. You don't have to do the same sort of thing — one person could be tidying up while the other finishes their homework, for instance — but both activities need to be quiet enough not to disturb the other.

When the timer goes off, you can check in and tell each other what you've got done. Whatever progress you've both made, congratulate each other for it! If you both want to, you could start another body doubling session after a quick break.

Brain break
Facts, games and ADHD-friendly activities to give your brain a rest

 Blue whales mostly eat teeny-tiny crustaceans called krill — but they eat a lot of them! In fact, they eat as much food in a single day as an average human might in 30 years or more.

 Set a timer for one minute. Before it goes off, how many words can you think of that start and end with the same letter — like 'roar', 'pip' or 'silliness'? Count on your fingers as you go!

It feels like everyone has ADHD! Isn't it overdiagnosed now?

Experts actually think that ADHD is still underdiagnosed, even in countries with higher rates, despite an increase in ADHD **diagnoses** in recent years. It's more that ADHD was so under-diagnosed in the past that, to some people, this increase seems like it must be an incorrectly big jump.

Some reasons for this recent increase are thought to include a wider awareness of ADHD and its **symptoms**, a better understanding of how ADHD shows up in girls and women, and improved methods for diagnosing ADHD.

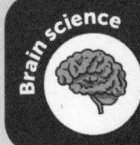
One of the first-known mentions of a medical condition that appears similar to ADHD was in 1798. Sir Alexander Crichton, a Scottish doctor, wrote about people having difficulty focusing their attention on particular tasks or activities, and being **impulsive** and restless.

Side quest

Draw a blue whale! Just follow the steps below. Maybe you could draw it huuuuge on a massive piece of paper or a flattened-out cardboard box, for a more realistic whale effect!

1. Draw the body and mouth

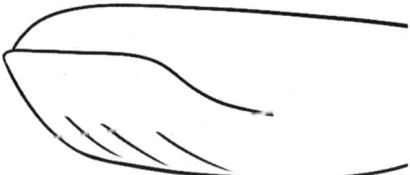

2. Draw the eye

Did you know?

A blue whale's blood vessels are so wide that you could fit a toddler into the biggest one – but don't try!

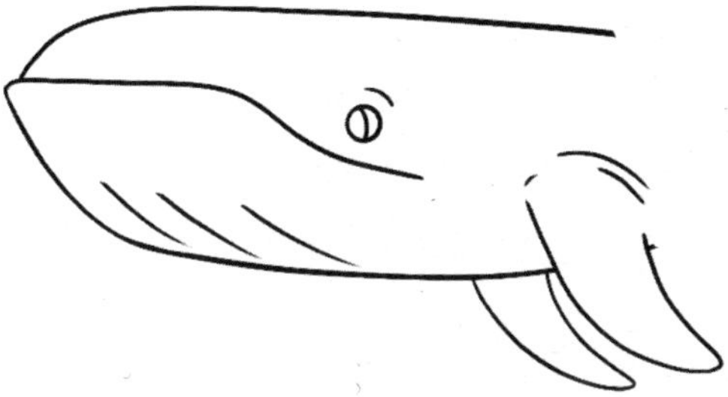

3. Draw the fins

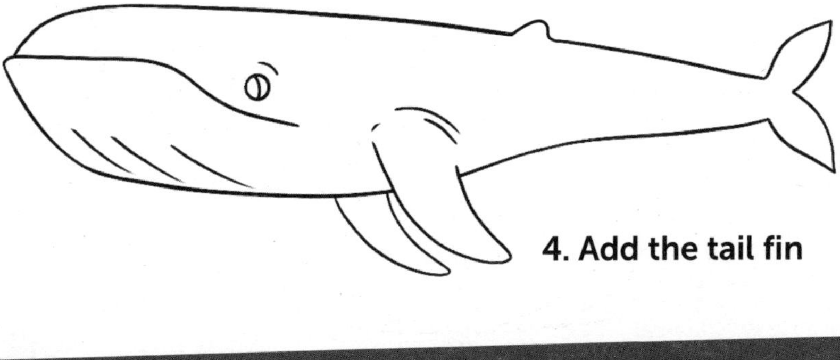

4. Add the tail fin

Chapter twelve
Raccoon

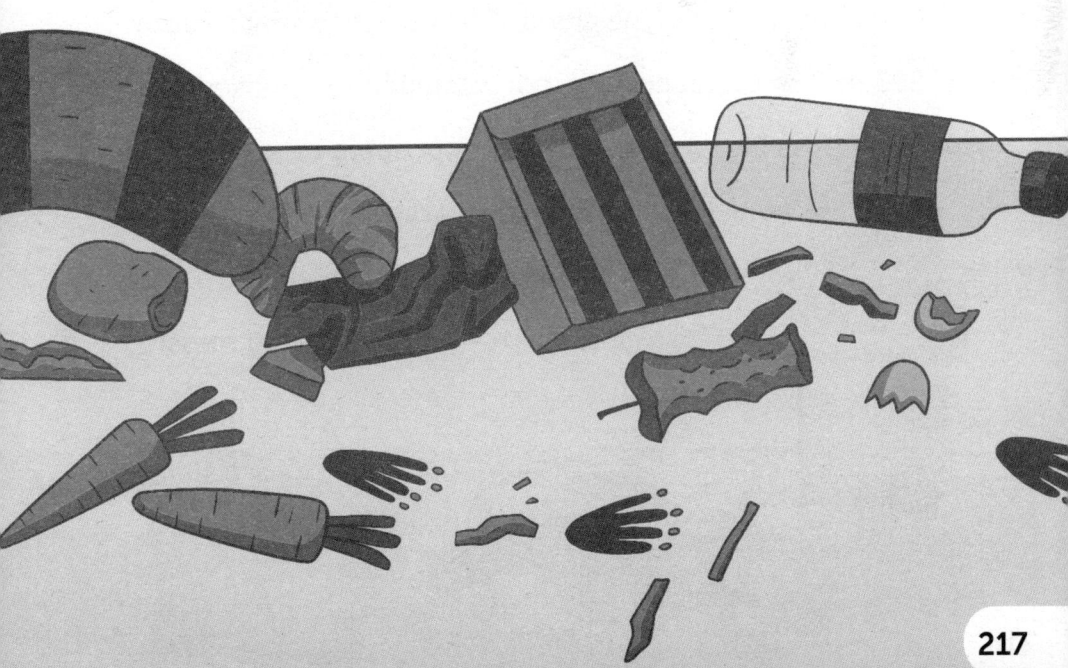

Raccoon

Being messily brilliant

Strength

Raccoons are incredibly clever animals that have adapted well to living in towns and cities. Studies suggest that they are much smarter than cats or dogs – so smart that they often escape from the testing centres where scientists are setting them puzzles to solve!

These curious, cunning (and pretty cute!) critters can be so good at creative problem-solving that they actually outsmart humans. The city of Toronto once spent about $23 million on raccoon-proof waste bins, supposedly impossible to open without opposable thumbs (which humans have and raccoons don't). But some raccoons STILL managed to get into them – and make a big mess!

Research suggests that people with ADHD can be highly innovative. We typically do very well at tests for divergent thinking (see page 151), coming up with a wider and more creative range of solutions to a single problem. We also seem to have a particular knack for problem-solving in unique ways, using instinct (an inner sense of what feels right) rather than analysis (logically working through information to find a solution).

ADHDers' problem-solving brilliance often doesn't look neat and tidy, and our creative solutions might be so out of the ordinary that some people misunderstand them. But that doesn't mean we're wrong! Embracing the way our brains seem to naturally work best, rather than forcing them to stick to the way we think we're 'supposed' to do or think about something, can spark wonderfully original ideas — perhaps, one day, even world-changing ones!

Struggle

Raccoons are clever, creative problem-solvers but they are also M-E-S-S-Y! Their curiosity and ingenuity lead them into all sorts of unexpected places, from people's attics to their fridges. They often leave food scraps, dirty paw prints, scratches, torn-up surfaces and more behind them as they go.

For many **ADHDers** (like me!), being neat, tidy and organised doesn't always come naturally. This can cause us all sorts of issues – from losing important things and running late because we can't find them, to feeling so embarrassed about our messy room that we don't invite friends over. The 'visual clutter' of a messy space can also make lots of us feel stressed and **overwhelmed**.

It's not that we don't want or care about things being tidy, or that we are being lazy. Our brains can find an instruction like 'Tidy your room' overwhelming because it actually includes lots of different tasks.

Keeping things clean, tidy and organised typically requires many different processes that can overwhelm ADHDers' brains. We may struggle with **executive functions** (see page 197) – skills that help with **prioritising** tasks, making decisions, starting and finishing tasks, managing our time and using our **working memory** to hold onto the information we need to complete a task.

This may mean that we 'freeze', wanting to get everything done but finding ourselves unable to because our brain is so overloaded and confused by what we're asking of it. We may also find it so hard to keep things tidy day to day that there is a big, daunting mess by the time we try to tackle it.

Tidying my room

☐ 1. Clearing old cups and plates
☐ 2. Picking up rubbish
☐ 3. Putting away clothes in drawers
☐ 4. Hanging up other clothes
☐ 5. Sorting out stack of papers
☐ 6. Putting away books
☐ 7. Sorting out school bag

Our brains' differences in how we manage attention and resist **impulsivity** can also mean that we get easily distracted while tidying, or may find ourselves **hyperfocusing** on one tiny part of what needs to be done. This could mean that an hour later, our room still looks a total mess but we've perfectly re-organised a bookshelf by colour or expertly cleaned one pair of trainers so they look sparkling new!

Some **ADHDers** may worry so much about being messy, and feel so ashamed about it, that we spend huge amounts of time and energy keeping everything perfectly neat. **Masking** (see page 110) our ADHD **traits** in this way is often stressful and exhausting to keep up.

Working with your brain

It's worth remembering that everyone has their own idea of what 'messy' looks like, and is comfortable with different levels of neatness and organisation. This is as true for work and problem-solving as it is for keeping a room, a school bag or anything else tidy.

If a process or system works for our brain, and makes it easier to get things done, does it matter if it doesn't look perfect or make complete sense to others?

Trying to force ourselves to do things the so-called 'right' way can often mean they don't get done at all. Instead, we can try to better understand and trust how we like to think, work and live, and use our creative problem-solving to find solutions to fit our unique set of needs.

People with ADHD are all different. Some can thrive in 'organised chaos', which may look like a total mess to others but is actually made up of systems that work well for them. If it's not unsafe, unhygienic or negatively affecting them or others (for example, a sibling sharing the room), then maybe this doesn't need to change!

However, there are many ADHDers (I'm one of them) who feel a lot calmer and manage

THIS IS MY 'CLOTHES-I'VE-WORN-BUT-DON'T-NEED-TO-WASH' PILE

daily demands a lot better when things are reasonably clean, tidy and organised. That doesn't mean we necessarily find it easier to keep things like this, though!

Here are some ideas for working with your brain to find and keep up (with some natural ups and downs) a level of tidiness and organisation that suits you and your life (people without ADHD might even find them helpful, too):

Break down general tasks like 'Tidy your room' or 'Organise your schoolwork' into smaller, more achievable tasks to help support your brain and stop it feeling so stressed, confused and **overwhelmed**. See pages 204–206 for more details on how to do this, and how to use timed bursts of effort to get things done.

Make your efforts at tidiness fit your current habits as much as possible, rather than trying to force your brain to adopt lots of new ones. For example, if you always dump stuff in a particular spot when you come in, because it feels too much to put it away 'properly', could you put a basket or hook there so it's neater?

When there isn't a clear place to put something, this adds an unhelpful extra layer of **executive function** to a tidying task. Not only are we asking our brain to put something away, we're also asking it to decide on the best place for it to go. Often, this feels overwhelming, so the object ends up on the floor or nearest surface, or maybe pushed out of sight in a random drawer or folder. So why not try labelling certain areas, or choosing particular drawers for certain items? You could even use a label-maker to help so you always know where certain objects live.

ART SUPPLIES

For example, there are sometimes clothes we've worn that could be worn again without washing. They don't fit neatly into either the 'put away' or 'washing' category so can often end up on the floor, bed or desk, where they're in the way. Could they have their own chair or open-top box instead?

Talking with a trusted adult or friend about any obstacles you face while tidying can make things easier over time. It may help you realise where you don't know how to tidy or organise certain things, or where the current solution isn't working and could be improved (perhaps it involves too many steps?).

Ask this person to sit with you and listen while you tidy your room, your schoolwork, your backpack, your computer files or anything else that you would like to be less messy. When you come to a tricky part, talk it through and try to work out a simple solution together.

Many ADHDers find body doubling helpful to get tasks done. Learn more about it on page 210.

ADHDers sometimes leave things out, rather than putting them away in cupboards and drawers, because our memory differences can mean that we forget about things we don't see often. However, if everything is out, then we might not notice the things we want to see! You could ask a trusted adult to help you make lists of what's in drawers, cupboards, boxes and so on, and stick labels on the outside to remind you what's inside. Then you can just leave a few things out, with less clutter around.

Daily life can end up being pretty tiring for our brains, as our **executive function** challenges can mean we have to make a huge effort to complete everyday tasks. Trying to be perfectly tidy and organised all day on top of this can just be too much. What can be helpful is to aim for 'better than nothing', rather than perfection.

For example, perfection might be taking all handout sheets at the end of a class and slotting them neatly into empty sleeves in the right section of a colour-coded ring binder. Lovely and achievable for some people, but at school, I would have had about as much chance of keeping this up all day as of growing wings and flying to the Moon. Yet I tried, and any sheets I received actually ended up stuffed into my bag at the last moment, arriving home crumpled, torn and occasionally covered in goo from an old, forgotten banana. And I felt so frustrated and ashamed with myself for not living up to the impossible standards that I'd set.

What if instead I'd had a single, open-top folder that I could leave in my bag and slide any papers straight into, all mixed in together? I probably could have managed that. It's not 'perfect', but the best system is the one that actually works.

Some people reading the last point may be thinking, *OK sure, but what about when you keep stuffing that one folder with sheets until it breaks, or you need to find something and all the subject sheets are mixed up together and out of order?* And you're right! Keeping things tidy and organised all day in real time can be exhausting, asking too much of our overloaded brains. So what can be really helpful is to let things slide a bit, knowing that you'll have a chance to get them sorted later.

Short daily and weekly check-ins, supported by a trusted adult, can be so helpful. Among other things, they're a chance to keep things from getting so messy that it makes other tasks harder than they need to be. They also set up a realistic expectation that you're not going to keep things neat all the time, and that's fine! The check-ins are an opportunity to get back on track and maintain a helpful level of tidiness and organisation, whatever that means to you. Read more about this on pages 249–257.

It's generally a lot easier to keep things tidy and uncluttered when you have less stuff! Ask a trusted adult to help you learn more about **minimalism**, which some **ADHDers** find very helpful.

Draw a grid of four squares. Fill each square with a pattern made of circles, triangles, squares or wavy lines. Colour them in if you like!

You can try drawing more squares and filling them with the same patterns, or totally different ones.

Brain break

Facts, games and ADHD-friendly activities to give your brain a rest

Some studies suggest that raccoons living in cities and towns may be better at problem-solving than those in the countryside. They think this is because urban and suburban environments, with all their human-created obstacles, give raccoons more everyday challenges. They're constantly learning new things, which seems to make them more used to unfamiliar problems and better at solving them.

WARNING: Never get close to a raccoon – or its poo. Raccoons can carry deadly diseases, such as rabies and raccoon roundworm, that can infect humans too.

IRRITATING ADHD QUESTIONS:

No offence, but isn't ADHD just an excuse for being lazy?

It can be more difficult for some people to understand and empathise with what are known as 'invisible disabilities', such as ADHD, than with clear physical disabilities. But it's really a question of trust and respect.

If someone tells you that they experience the world differently, and put in lots of effort every day to deal with challenges that you may not have yourself, you can choose to believe them – even if you can't imagine exactly what that feels like.

Side quest

Set a timer for one minute and try to fill a page with (regular-sized) writing. Write whatever pops into your head — spelling and handwriting don't matter and it doesn't even have to make sense!

When the timer goes off, look back at what you wrote about — is it surprising? Free writing can be really interesting! If you liked it, you can keep going for another minute.

Did you know?

Raccoons have been observed dunking their food into water before eating it, but do you know why? They're not washing it — they're checking if it's good to eat! Raccoons have super-sensitive front paws, with sensory nerves that work even better in water. With wet paws, they can learn more about a food's size, texture, temperature and so on, and decide if it seems like a safe, tasty treat!

Do you ever find yourself clenching your jaw or grinding your teeth? Were you maybe doing it right then, until you read this and remembered to relax your jaw?! (I did just that when I was writing this!)

Studies have found a strong link between bruxism – jaw-clenching and tooth-grinding – and ADHD. Bruxism is common among children and teenagers, and it can negatively affect sleep, which may make ADHD **symptoms** more noticeable.

If you think this is happening to you, or you get jaw and tooth pain, you can check with your dentist. It can be linked to stress (see pages 58–64 for some ideas about how to relax).

Conclusion and extra resources

What do ADHDers and octopuses have in common?

You might not immediately relate to a squishy, slimy undersea creature that has three hearts, eight suction-cup-covered arms and the ability to change colour in seconds – but hear me out!

For a very long time, humans massively underestimated how clever octopuses are. Their brains have evolved so differently to ours, and their behaviours are so unfamiliar, that even experts didn't usually understand or recognise their complex brilliance. It just didn't match up to what they expected intelligence to look like – that is, something much more similar to their own mammal brain and its particular strengths.

However, since science has started taking a more open-minded approach to octopuses, we've discovered just how incredible these creatures really are. In fact, one leading biologist has said that if humans ever die out, then octopuses might be the next species to take over Earth!

ADHD brains have also long been misunderstood and underappreciated, because they don't follow all the 'rules' of how a **neurotypical** brain is expected to work. The focus has traditionally been – and often still is – on what our brains can find particularly challenging. But researchers are now finding out more and more about what **ADHDers** excel at, and better understanding how our brains approach things differently and just as successfully as neurotypical people (if not more so!)

Alongside this, there's a growing understanding of how hard people with ADHD have to work just to get by in a world generally built to suit neurotypical strengths, needs and preferences. We have to do everything that neurotypical people do PLUS constantly work out our own ADHD-friendly ways to function when the typical ways of doing things don't work for us! This means that judging ourselves by **neurotypical** standards is even more unfair and unhelpful than it first seems.

It wasn't until I got my ADHD **diagnosis** that I really understood how differently my brain worked compared to so many people's — that the wild, rebellious rollercoaster of my brain's day-to-day was not a universal experience, and that what I found easy or near-impossible often varied quite dramatically from what was considered 'typical'. Learning to understand and work with my ADHD brain, rather than harshly judging it and fighting against it, has been a truly life-changing experience. There are still things I find difficult, of course, but I'm more ready for them now and can help myself with all sorts of tools and strategies that actually work for me (most of the time!)

I can also recognise and better appreciate some of my strengths, which lots of **ADHDers** seem to share —

from my creativity and endless curiosity to my friendly chattiness and inability to accept 'that's just how things are' as an excuse for hurting people and the planet. It might feel odd at first, or even boastful, to think about your own strengths, but please try to do this regularly, too!

You could even write a list in a notebook or digital note – not to show anyone else if you don't want to, but just to look at and add to when you remember. As people with ADHD can often receive so many negative messages from society, recognising and valuing our individual strengths can help to balance things out and remind us how these strengths can support us through trickier times.

I AM KIND.
I AM CREATIVE.
I STAND UP
FOR WHAT I
BELIEVE IN.

I really hope that this book has helped you better understand and appreciate your ADHD brain in all its exciting, frustrating, joyful, confusing glory. Being an **ADHDer** isn't always easy, that's for sure, but you and your uniquely brilliant brain have so much to offer. So take care, ask for the support you need and remember that you're not alone. There are millions of fellow ADHDers, including me, all around the world – and we're all learning how to work with our WILD and WONDERFUL brains!

Over the next few pages, you'll find some extra resources to help you develop your **growth mindset**, self-compassion and 'scaffolding' systems to help you and your ADHD brain thrive.

Remember: everyone's brain and life is different, so feel free to try things out and see what works best for you!

Growth mindset and self-compassion

Growth mindset

We often think and talk about intelligence and abilities as if they are stuck the way they are, and will be forever. This is called a fixed mindset, and it can make us feel like there's no point in even trying. We may also worry about making mistakes, seeing them as 'proof' that we'll never be as capable as we should be.

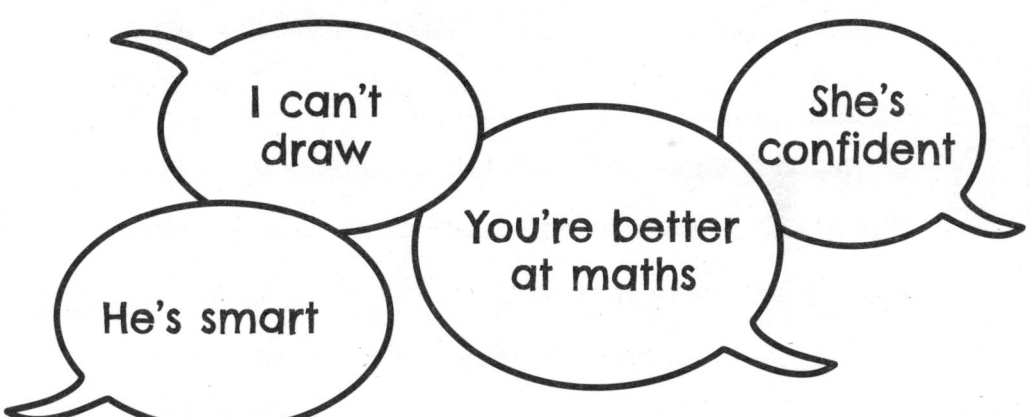

However, scientific studies have shown that our brains are always growing and changing, and keep on developing throughout our lives. Every brain has billions of **neurons**, cells that pass messages along their connections, and our thoughts and actions can help strengthen these existing connections and build new ones. Thinking about our brains in this way – and understanding that they can learn and grow from taking on new challenges and making mistakes – is known as a **growth mindset**.

Brain science

The theory of fixed and growth mindsets was developed by the psychologist Dr Carol Dweck.

Developing a growth mindset doesn't mean pretending that ADHD differences don't exist, or will stop affecting us if we just put in enough effort. Not at all! It's about working with our brains as they are, accepting that some things will feel different or come easier to others, and being willing to keep trying. It's about learning from experiences that we find challenging, rather than judging ourselves harshly and giving up altogether.

This isn't always easy but the results can be incredible, and it helps us to approach life — and think about ourselves — in a generally more positive, open-minded way.

The power of 'yet'

A good place to start is with the word 'yet'! Whenever you catch yourself thinking, 'I can't do this', try adding on 'yet'. This can encourage you to keep putting in the effort and working towards your goal.

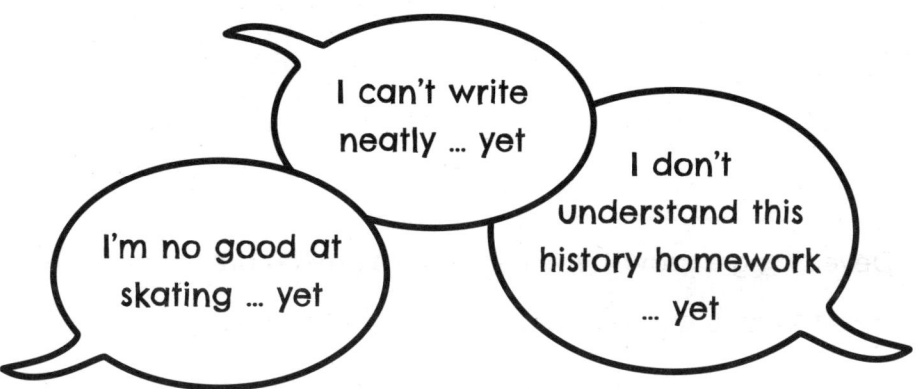

Of course, you don't have to do this all on your own. Part of learning and growing is asking for help and support when you need it, not just keeping on and on until you **burn out**.

Self-compassion

Self-compassion means being kind to yourself, especially when you feel that you've failed at something or made a mistake. Many people find it difficult to be self-compassionate and to treat themselves with the same gentleness and understanding that they would show a friend.

Multiple scientific studies have suggested that people with ADHD experience low self-compassion in particular. This can really affect our **mental health** and enjoyment of life.

Practising self-compassion can support us in developing a **growth mindset**, by helping us feel safer to make mistakes and learn from them. We can remind ourselves that everyone makes mistakes, that it's a shared part of being human, and that doing something wrong – or not as well as we'd hoped – doesn't make us a bad or rubbish person.

GOOD JOB!

Here are three simple ways to start building the habit of self-compassion:

1. 'Ouch!': When you notice that you're criticising yourself, stop and acknowledge it. Some people like to say 'Ouch!' or 'That's not very nice!' in their head – or even out loud. This can interrupt your harsh train of thought. Then, you can reframe it in a more **compassionate** way and think about what you could learn from it. For example, you might think:

I got the lowest mark of all my friends for my presentation. I'm so stupid and embarrassing!

But tell yourself 'ouch!' and reframe it as:

I was really worried about the presentation and I put off working on it until the last moment. Then I didn't feel prepared, which made me more nervous. But I'm allowed to have difficult feelings and make mistakes, just like everyone else. I will ask for help next time.

2. Be a friend: When you catch yourself being mean or overly harsh to yourself, imagine you're talking to a friend. Do you think it would be OK to talk to them like that? How do you think it would make them feel? Well, you're human too, and you deserve the same kindness and understanding that you'd show to your friend!

Think about what you might say to a friend in your position, whether you're feeling bad about something or struggling with a problem. Then say that to yourself instead! It can be helpful to actually write it down in a note, with their name at the top, and then replace your name with theirs once you've finished writing.

3. Give yourself the good things: We can often be more critical of ourselves than of others because, deep down, we may feel that we're not as good as them. That anything we don't do exactly as we'd hoped is 'proof' of this, and that it means we don't deserve nice treatment like others do. For people belonging to **marginalised** groups, including **neurodivergent** people such as **ADHDers** and **AuDHDers**, this may come — at least in part — from unknowingly absorbing society's incorrect messages that certain ways of existing as a human are 'better' than our own.

Try saying 'I deserve good things', either in your head or out loud, right now. How does it feel? Weird? Uncomfortable? Nice? Maybe there's a voice pushing back on the statement, saying 'No, you don't'? Perhaps you're feeling all of these things at once?

Try repeating this to yourself a few more times, and writing it down and placing it somewhere you'll see it regularly. Then, try saying it and doing something that you enjoy, or that makes you feel good — this is something that will be personal to you, but here are some ideas to get you started:

- listening to your favourite music
- kicking a ball around with a sibling or friend
- reading your favourite book
- chatting or playing with a friend
- asking a parent or carer for a hug

You're telling your brain that you deserve good things, and *then* showing it this is true by doing something nice for yourself. Talk with a trusted adult about adding this into your daily or weekly routine, so you get plenty of practice – and more of the good things you deserve!

Scaffolding

You've seen scaffolding on a building, right? A frame of boards and poles that supports people working high up. Now imagine that support, but for your brain!

Scaffolding is a personalised set of routines and systems that support **ADHDers** in areas they might find difficult (such as organisation or planning) and add structure to their daily lives, helping them to thrive.

All of us have different strengths and challenges, so no one's scaffolding will look exactly the same. You also don't have to set up or manage your scaffolding alone – ask a trusted adult to help you develop your system and help you keep it going. If you need extra support for memory differences, some examples of scaffolding may include:

A (digital or paper) calendar: This might include appointments, deadlines and other events to remember (from a football match to a friend's birthday party).

A (digital or paper) copy of your typical weekly/ two-weekly schedule: This information can go in your calendar but it's easy to miss things with too much written for each day, so it may help to keep basic details in your calendar (like school start and end times, not individual classes) and more detail in this schedule.

A (digital or paper) task list: This might include both one-off and regular tasks. If you prefer, you could add these tasks straight into your calendar or schedule.

Checklists for things you do regularly: For example, packing your bag for school, packing an extra bag for football practice, cleaning your room, getting ready in the morning, getting ready for bed. (Note: if it makes you feel silly to write these checklists because you think you should 'just remember', please know that I – a fully grown adult and mum – have about twenty on my phone that I refer to ALL THE TIME.)

Tidying my room
- [ ] 1. Clearing old cups and plates
- [ ] 2. Picking up rubbish
- [ ] 3. Putting away clothes in drawers

A (paper or digital note) cheat sheet: Use this for important information that you use regularly and find hard to remember. Just make sure that any personal information is kept safe and secure.

If you prefer paper to digital, you can buy a planner with space for all of the features above. It helps keep everything together, but some people prefer keeping each part separate.

You can also have a mix of paper and digital (I do), for example a digital calendar and paper task list. Just try to keep things as simple as possible to avoid confusion. See what works best for you!

It's important to put dates and tasks straight into your calendar or task list right away, before you forget them! If for some reason you don't have your calendar or task list with you, a pocket notebook can be a helpful 'holding space' for quick notes until you can transfer them into your scaffolding systems.

Some information isn't a task, details of an event, or anything else to use immediately or regularly. Information like this that you don't want to forget — anything from interesting facts to fun activities you'd like to try some day — can go into a separate notebook or digital file.

You could even split up the notebook or digital file into different pages or sections to make it easier to look things up in future. Just keep it somewhere easily visible so you don't completely forget about it. (I have done this myself!)

Reviews

The only way that my scaffolding stays clear and up to date, and therefore useful, is by scheduling in quick reviews at a set time each day and week.

Ask a trusted adult to find a regular time to do these reviews with you. Having another person to prompt you will help make these reviews a habit, and they'll be aware of any times when you have a lot on and need support.

It can be helpful to tie a new habit you want to start to something that you already do regularly. For example, if you always have a snack when you get home from school (or after-school club), maybe you could do your quick daily review while – or just after – eating your snack.

You can also help yourself look forward to the review by doing something fun straight afterwards, whatever that might be for you, or by using a sticker chart for a quick reward and **dopamine** boost!

Remember, these short check-ins are not about testing or judging you in any way! They're about supporting you, helping you keep track of important things, and making your daily life easier by stopping things from getting too overwhelming or messy.

Daily

A daily review only needs to take five minutes. Take a quick look over your day (calendar, daily task list), including anything in your pocket notebook or other loose notes in your pocket or bag.

Then look ahead at tomorrow. Is there anything out of the ordinary happening tomorrow? Have you got everything you need ready and in your bag? Are there any extra tasks that need to go on tomorrow's task list? Quickly prep now, with your trusted adult, so you're all set.

Weekly

Take a look over the past week (calendar, weekly schedule, task list). Is there anything that didn't happen, that needs doing this week? Look ahead to next week, and think about anything you need to do or prepare for. Any differences to your routine? Any project deadlines, exams or after-school events? A friend's birthday that you want to make or buy a present for? Add it to the calendar, task list or the next weekly schedule.

If you are doing progress check-ins (see page 76) with a trusted adult, it might be helpful to do them at the same time as this weekly review. Then you'll have one less thing to remember!

Reminders

Another thing I do to help me keep on top of my scaffolding is set up reminders. These can be digital or you can ask someone to help you remember until you get used to always checking something at the same time every day. (It's OK if it takes a while to form the habit!)

Digital

If your trusted adult sets up digital scaffolding systems for you – for instance, a calendar and a to-do list app on a tablet – then you can ask them to set up alerts to remind you of events, tasks and so on.

It can also help to set up extra alerts ahead of this actual time to remind you, for example, to pack something in your bag, walk to the school bus stop, or start a school project with enough time before the deadline. Ask a trusted adult to help you with this, as they can help you work out how much time things might take.

On many to-do list apps, you can set up recurring tasks, with reminders every week, month or so on for things that you need to do regularly.

Paper

Paper scaffolding systems don't give you automatic alerts like digital ones can, so the daily and weekly reviews we looked at earlier in this section are extra-important to remind you of what's coming up.

You could also ask a trusted adult to remind you if you're not using a digital system.

Try to also get in the habit of quickly checking your calendar/schedule/task list through the day, to give you multiple reminders. Keep it somewhere where you'll see it all the time, with the pages you need open or folded down at the corners, so this is as easy as possible for your brain.

Don't worry if your scaffolding system gets a bit messy or if you skip a few reviews — it's totally normal! When you notice this happening, don't be hard on yourself, as it can actually make it harder to get started again because your brain typically tries to avoid things it associates with difficult feelings.

Just try to pick up where you left off, and talk with a trusted adult about helping to keep you on track — including adjusting your scaffolding if needed, so it feels as simple and helpful as possible.

Glossary

adaptability – ability to change how you do things to suit different situations

ADHDer – an informal/non-medical way of describing someone who has ADHD

advocate – to stand up for yourself or others in order to receive fair treatment

amygdala – a part of your brain that helps you notice and react to strong feelings

AuDHD –an informal term for someone who is autistic and also has ADHD

auditory processing disorder – a condition that means you can have difficulty understanding the sounds you hear, including spoken words

authority – anyone who is in charge of others, or has the power to set rules

autism – an autistic person may communicate, interact with others and experience the world differently to a non-autistic person. Autistic people may consider themselves neurodivergent

boundaries – limits that you set for yourself to help protect your safety, health and happiness

brain dump – unloading all of your thoughts, ideas, worries, tasks and anything else on your mind onto paper (or a digital document). For more information, turn to page 10

burnout – feeling extremely tired, empty and unable to do anything more

Civil Rights movement – a struggle by Black Americans for equal rights and an end to racial discrimination

combined type ADHD – people with this type of ADHD have both inattentive and hyperactive–impulsive traits

compassion – being kind and caring to someone who is upset or in a difficult situation. Self-compassion means showing this kind of kindness and care to yourself

controversial – something about which people often have strong, very different feelings and opinions

default mode network (DMN) – certain parts of your brain that work together to allow you to reflect on your own thoughts and engage with imagination and ideas

diagnosis – when a doctor, or other health professional, officially identifies that someone has a particular condition (such as ADHD)

dopamine – a chemical made in the human body that helps with focus and motivation. People with ADHD often experience an imbalance of dopamine levels in the brain, which can push us to seek out more

dyscalculia – a condition that affects a person's ability to understand and work with numbers

dyslexia – a condition that affects a person's ability to understand and process language and information

dyspraxia – a condition that affects a person's physical movements and co-ordination

empathy – the skill of imagining how others might feel and trying to understand their feelings, even if you don't agree with them or are in a very different situation to them

executive functions – complex mental processes and abilities that are involved in planning, decision-making, organisation, focusing attention and more

flow state – when you are absorbed in a task or activity, or 'in the zone' as it's sometimes known, and you don't feel distracted or like you want to stop

foraging – going from place to place looking for food, or other useful things

fulfilling – something that feels satisfying and worthwhile

genetics – the science of how different traits – from eye colour to some medical conditions – can be passed down from parent to child through our genes, which are tiny parts of our body's cells

growth mindset – thinking about your brain as being able to change and grow, rather than being fixed as it is

hunter-gatherer – a person who gets their food by hunting wild animals and searching for edible wild plants rather than by farming (there are lots of poisonous wild plants so don't ever try this yourself!)

hyperactive-impulsive ADHD – people with this type of ADHD may have very high energy and experience challenges with being still and with stopping themselves acting or speaking. For more information, turn to page 11

hyperactivity – being extremely active and energetic

hyperfocus – a state of intense concentration that can last for hours and hours on end

impulsivity – acting quickly, without thinking things through

inattentive ADHD – people with this type of ADHD may find it particularly hard to, for example, hold their attention on tasks and activities, resist distractions and remember what they're doing. For more information, turn to page 10

inquisitiveness – wanting to find out as much as you can about things

justice sensitivity – a tendency to have a strong sense of right and wrong, and to be unable to just ignore or accept when something seems unfair, like many people do

LGBTQIA+ — the letters stand for Lesbian, Gay, Bisexual, Transgender, Queer or Questioning, Intersex and Asexual. These terms can describe a person's gender or sexual orientation, and the '+' includes any other terms that people may use in this way

maladaptive daydreaming — a behaviour where someone regularly spends a huge amount of time daydreaming, getting so lost in their daydreams that it affects their daily life

marginalised — treated as if not important, and deliberately left out or pushed out

masking — hiding parts of yourself, including your ADHD traits, to fit in with others and avoid negative reactions

mental health — how someone is feeling in their mind and emotions

minimalism — a 'less is more' way of thinking, where people try to only buy and keep things they actually need or really care about

momentum — a sense that you're making progress, and that things are getting a bit quicker and easier as you go

motivation — the desire to do something or to work towards a goal

nervous system – your brain, spinal cord and nerves, working together to sense the world around you and react to it

neurodivergent – when someone thinks, learns or behaves differently to what society sees as 'typical'. People with ADHD may consider themselves neurodivergent. Neurodiversity is the idea that everyone's brain is different, and that we all experience and react to the world in different, equally valuable ways. Everyone is neurodiverse (including neurotypical people), but some people use this word in the same way as 'neurodivergent'

neuron – a type of cell in your brain and nervous system that sends and receives messages, allowing you to think, feel and move

neurotypical – when someone thinks, learns and/or behaves in ways that society sees as 'typical'

noradrenaline – a chemical made in the human body that helps with focus and motivation. It is also known as norepinephrine

obsessive-compulsive disorder (OCD) – a condition that affects a person's mental health, causing them to regularly have unpleasant, unwanted thoughts and to feel they have to do certain actions over and over again

overstimulated – when your brain feels overloaded by everything it's trying to take in, and you may feel stressed or upset

overwhelming – when it feels like there is too much happening at once, and your brain is too crowded with thoughts, feelings, things to do and so on

persecuted – treated cruelly and unfairly over a long time, often because of a certain identity or beliefs

perspective – your personal view or way of thinking about something

primate – an animal that belongs to the group of mammals that includes humans, monkeys, apes and more

prioritise – to put things in order of importance, often to then deal with the most important thing first

productive – doing or achieving a lot

rejection sensitivity – when someone feels so upset by rejection or criticism – whether real or imagined – that they feel incredibly intense emotional pain

resilient – an inner strength that can help us to handle life's challenges

self-esteem – how we feel about ourselves, and how valuable we think we are

social cues – ways people may communicate what they're thinking or how they're feeling to others, without stating this directly (such as facial expressions, body language or subtle conversational 'hints')

spontaneous – doing things without planning them, just because you feel like it in the moment

stimming – making repeating movements or sounds, with your body or objects, often without realising. Common stims (short for 'self-stimulatory behaviours') include playing with a pen, rocking, twirling your hair, tapping your foot or humming

sustainable – something that you can keep doing over a long time, without it harming you

symptom – a physical or mental effect or trait that someone experiences because of a medical condition

Tourette syndrome – a condition that causes people to make sudden, repeated sounds and movements, called tics. They do not choose to make them, and cannot control them

trait – a particular way that someone tends to think or behave

traumatic – when an event is very scary, upsetting and stressful

trigger – to cause a strong, often very challenging, emotional reaction

ultraviolet (UV) – a type of light that humans can't see, but some other animals can

unmasking – when you stop hiding parts of yourself, including your ADHD traits, to fit in with others

well-being – feeling healthy, comfortable and generally happy or content

working memory – how we hold recent information in our minds, often for only a short time, and then use it to complete a particular task

Thank yous

I'm so grateful to everyone who has worked so hard to bring this book to life!

Thank you so much to everyone at Bloomsbury — especially my editor Emily Ball, who so clearly understood right from the start what I wanted this book to be, and my designer, Katie Knutton, who made this book look so beautiful. Thanks also to Céline Culliford, Sophie Harrington and everyone else at Bloomsbury who was involved in the book for their brilliant work.

Huge thanks also to my agent, Lydia Silver, for her invaluable help and insight in turning my idea into a finished proposal. Big thanks too to Hannah Hirst-Dunton, Dr Valeria Parlatini, Lex Academic and, of course, Buse Kaçar for her fabulous illustrations!

Last but very much not least, thank you to my husband, David — for always being so patient and supportive, and for loving me and my wild brain just as we are.

Afterword

Your Wild and Wonderful Brain offers a practical, hands-on guide to ADHD for children and teens. By mapping symptoms onto relatable animal traits, the author brings real-world experience to life in bite-sized examples that help young people better understand their strengths, address challenges and **advocate** for themselves.

Descriptions and strategies are grounded in clear, accessible science and brain facts – an especially important feature given how common misinformation about ADHD remains. We strongly encourage readers to rely on reputable sources of information, such as trusted charities and NHS websites

If in doubt, especially regarding a potential diagnosis or treatment, please always speak with your trusted health professional.

Helping people with ADHD as part of my work is personally deeply rewarding. Many challenges can be reframed as strengths, and individuals can find education and career paths that better align with their skills and needs. This book brings young people and parents together on a shared journey to better understand ADHD and to help youths realise their full potential.

Dr Valeria Parlatini, MD, PhD, AFHEA, MRCPsych
Associate Professor/Hon. Consultant in Child and Adolescent Psychiatry, University of Southampton/Hampshire and IOW Healthcare NHS Foundation Trust
Visiting Senior Lecturer in Child and Adolescent Psychiatry, King's College London

About the author

Alice Harman loves writing fun, thoughtful non-fiction books that make big ideas feel exciting and easy to understand. She has written more than 50 children's books, about everything from modern art to outer space. Diving into so many different, fascinating subjects keeps her ADHD brain happy!

Alice's books have been translated into 15 languages, nominated for the UKLA and Blue Peter Book Awards, and featured in publications such as the *New York Times*. Alice is also an editor and author coach, helping other writers develop their own brilliant books. She lives in a pretty town in Derbyshire, UK, with her family and a very silly cat.

About the illustrator

Buse Kaçar is an illustrator from Istanbul, Turkey, currently based in Germany. She studied Plastic Arts and Painting for her bachelor's degree and later completed teacher training after graduating. Her work mainly focuses on children's toys, books and puzzles, and she also creates editorial illustrations. Through her art, Buse hopes to celebrate cultural diversity and contribute to a world that feels more open, inclusive and free from bias.

Growing up, Buse was inspired by the cartoons she loved watching as a child. She brings that same sense of warmth, playfulness and attention to detail into her own work, hoping readers will discover something new each time they return to it. Her illustrations have been featured in several international exhibitions and she was a finalist in the commercial category of the Golden Pinwheel 2023.